classic kitchen style

classic kitchen style

the essential handbook for a timeless design

by Mervyn Kaufman
and the editors of

Woman's Day Special Interest Publications

Copyright © 2008
Filipacchi Publishing, a division of
Hachette Filipacchi Media U.S., Inc.

First published in 2008 in the
United States of America by
Filipacchi Publishing
1633 Broadway
New York, NY 10019

Woman's Day Special Interest
Publication is a registered trademark
of Hachette Filipacchi Media U.S., Inc.

Editor: Jennifer Ladonne
Design: Patricia Fabricant
Production: Ed Barredo

ISBN: 1-933231-36-X

Printed in China

contents

introduction

What constitutes classic style? To some, it's note-for-note historical accuracy—faithful reproductions of a period look, whether it's American Colonial, French Country or English Victorian. There's a certain satisfaction in getting all the key details right, from an authentic color palette to specific wood species, to antique appliances.

Other people take a more relaxed view towards achieving a classic kitchen. For them, an artless assemblage of assorted familiar elements—wood cabinets, an apron sink, a cooking alcove—forms a timeless space that's more about comfort than correctness. In this interpretation, "classic" is as much an outlook as it is a look.

The rooms featured in this book embody both takes on the term. Writer and kitchen authority Mervyn Kaufman puts into words the grace these kitchens convey, and shares his extensive knowledge of the hows and whys of designing the classic kitchen that's right for you.

–Leslie Plummer Clagett
Editor, *Kitchens & Baths*
Woman's Day Special Interest Publications

traditional elegance

Details are the earmarks of traditional design.

Whether the influence is English or European, the

look can be seen in such details as turned legs,

elaborate moldings, cabinetry with raised or recessed

paneling, and finishes that point up the beauty of

grained wood. In a traditional kitchen, the cabinets

resemble fine furniture, and door and drawer

hardware reflect period style. Order and refinement

rule, and the kitchen's contents are mostly concealed.

This is not a place for a dog bed or cat-litter box.

uncluttered efficiency

Before: A lack of space and a dated look were two major problems with the previous kitchen. "We could barely move around the small prep area and the cramped breakfast space," Pat recalled.

Pat Vuocolo, a kitchen designer and owner of Kitchens By Vuocolo of West Chester, Pennsylvania, has created her share of attractive and functional kitchens for clients. So after a decade in her mid-1960s ranch-style home, she and her husband, Jerry, an avid cook, finally decided it was time to remodel their own small and dreary kitchen.

"Jerry and I have three grown children and seven grandchildren," Pat said. "I wanted a kitchen that we could all be comfortable in, and one that would also serve as a showcase when clients visit." (Homeowners considering her services are invited to tour Pat's kitchen to see how she dealt with her own design challenges.)

The 229-square-foot space was long, narrow, and difficult to work in. First on the list to be removed was a cumbersome peninsula that was out of proportion to the room. Then she added usable square footage by absorbing space from a nearby laundry area and removing an outside wall to build an extension at one end of the kitchen.

Opening the room at this end also gave Pat a chance to install casement windows, which she designed to run the length of the room and wrap around the two corners. Adding new windows not only expanded the outdoor view but also made it possible to fill the room with natural light.

Custom cherry cabinets replaced the standard maple models installed forty years ago. "The new cabinets were selected to provide generous storage space as well as add richness to the room," Pat explained. Paying close attention to the use of space, she utilized the design of her cabinets in the most efficient way possible: "We never really had a proper place to store all of our pots and pans. I wanted to create cabinets that would include plenty of custom-designed drawers."

An important component of the new kitchen is its 3-by-10-foot center island built from the same cherry used for the cabinets. "Having a small sink in the island makes preparing meals very easy," said Pat. One end of the island contains display cabinets; on the other

what was done

- Opened a wall at one end to expand the room
- Added 10 square feet of cabinet space
- Installed seven casement windows over the sink area
- Replaced old appliances with all-new professional-style models
- Created a new center island that includes an eating area

BELOW, LEFT: The 229-square-foot kitchen was narrow and dominated by a large peninsula that was out of proportion to the rest of the room.

BELOW, RIGHT: Relocating appliances and eliminating one wall improved the storage capacity and efficiency of the new kitchen.

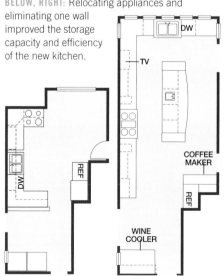

OPPOSITE; TOP, LEFT: Slide-out spice cabinets on each side of the hearth keep everything organized and allow for a quick inside search. A small drawer under each spice rack holds pot holders and oven mitts.

OPPOSITE; BOTTOM, LEFT: A custom hutch with a built-in coffee/cappuccino maker solves numerous storage issues. "It's such a treat to serve a choice of coffees any time of day," Pat explained. "I also included storage cabinets in the hutch for dishes and drawers for utensils. Everything I'll ever need is right there."

OPPOSITE; TOP, RIGHT: With a built-in wine cooler, open display shelves, and two roomy base cabinets, the new bar is a popular spot for guests. "We wanted an area where people could walk over to grab a drink, but we wanted it out of the way," the designer explained.

OPPOSITE; BOTTOM, RIGHT: Creating built-in spaces for small appliances can be a great way to conserve counter space. Here, a TV on a swivel stand is concealed inside a cabinet to the right of the hearth. "Jerry loves to watch his cooking shows while he works," said Pat.

end, open shelves provide space for cookbooks. The island is designed to accommodate four iron-backed chairs plus enough counter space for quick meals. Cream-colored granite with flecks of gold, brown, and black was used for the island's top and the surrounding counters. Pat also selected cream-colored porcelain tile in varying sizes for the floor. Because the kitchen is long and narrow—12½ feet at its widest point—Pat decided to stagger the floor tiles to create an optical illusion and eliminate a long railroad effect.

Improved lighting—well-placed recessed fixtures, low-voltage under-cabinet lighting, and a three-light, Mediterranean-style pendant fixture—now illuminates the clutter-free space.

Pat's creative spark has imbued the new 355-square-foot space with airiness and efficiency. It is a kitchen functional enough for two people to work in at the same time, and comfortable enough to be a gathering spot for the entire family.

finishing touches

Clearing a counter. The sleek design of a built-in coffee system (left) could blend with your kitchen's decor and provide sophisticated coffee options.

Hidden agenda. Incorporating a top pullout pantry into your kitchen redesign (right) could create eye-level organization of food products and a host of other kitchen essentials.

ABOVE, LEFT: The new sink has counter space on both sides and dishwasher drawers within easy reach. "I also added a built-in soap dispenser to eliminate clutter on the counter," said Pat.

dealing with size

ABOVE: An abundance of details—dentils and corbels—is the cabinets' crowning glory. The elaborate molding was built up layer by layer.

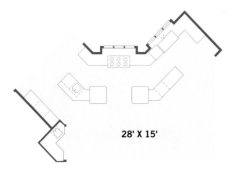

28' X 15'

ABOVE: The large kitchen has a hinged floor plan, making traffic flow and appliance placement especially critical to its functionality.

This kitchen was too big. Of course, most people wish they had that problem. But with a crook in the middle of the room, the space's commodious size was more a liability than a luxury. To keep the cooks from having to dash from one end of the room to the other, Cameron Snyder, CKD, of Kitchen Concepts, in Norwell, Massachusetts, devised an ingenious arrangement, one that is anchored by twin islands and a show-stopping central cooking zone.

The room is the way it is because that's how Art and Debbie Avila designed their new residence in Cohasset, Massachusetts. Art has been building homes for more than two decades, and the couple finally decided to create a house for themselves and their children. Thus began the madness.

"We had been doing them for other people for so long," Debbie said, "that from the second we decided to build a home for ourselves, we really lived it. We didn't talk about anything else! And we both knew that the kitchen would be the core of the house."

This shopworn remodeling axiom rang especially true for the couple. "Our house is more or less U-shaped

in plan. The kitchen is literally in the center of that U."

When they finished designing the house, they realized they would have a tough time coming up with a functional space, what with the bend in the middle of it. If you asked Snyder, he would tell you that wasn't the biggest challenge he faced.

"Debbie had some very specific details she wanted to incorporate in the room," he recalled. "She had put together a scrapbook of elements she wanted to use."

Debbie acknowledged that she did her homework and voiced her desires: "I pored through magazines and cut out pictures—certain kinds of mullioned doors, Gothic grilles. Whenever I saw something I liked, I ripped it out for my files. 'I want these feet. I want those corbels. I want to use interior columns wherever it's possible to find places for them.'"

While small touches like these give the kitchen a large part of its elegant character, ultimately the double islands and towering cooking alcove are the touchstones of the room's overall

OPPOSITE: A matching pair of split-level islands act as both boundary and gateway to the kitchen.

LEFT: Curved shapes—windows, counters, shelf openings, cabinet grilles—work together to counterbalance the kitchen's angular quality.

BOTTOM, LEFT: The undeniable focus of the room is the double-height cooking niche that occupies the central pivot point of the kitchen.

BELOW: With the main sink around a corner, having a pot-filler at the range was a necessity.

design. Debbie maintained, "Cameron dramatically changed the layout; when visitors come into the kitchen from the foyer, it's just an amazing experience for them."

The space has other guest-friendly considerations. "Even when there are fifteen people in the kitchen, it's a breeze," Debbie said. "People put their drinks on the raised parts of the islands, and we serve food on the islands' long lower lengths.

"At our last gathering, my husband suddenly asked me, 'Can you believe how well this kitchen works?'"

Before? Probably no. After the renovation? Absolutely yes.

RIGHT: The "hot" island facing the range is home to a warming drawer and a microwave.

BELOW: In the grandly scaled room, the primary light source is the windows. Recessed ceiling fixtures add overall illumination, and chandeliers provide a sparkly supplement.

a welcome change

By the time homeowners Rocky and Brett Parra welcomed a fourth child into their Pensacola, Florida, home, they knew for certain that their kitchen needed to expand right along with their family.

Held back by outmoded appliances, a wallpapered soffit that bisected the low ceiling, and a one-cook floor plan, the space begged for an overhaul. The Parras looked to designer Cheryl Kees, of In Detail, in Pensacola, to bring their kitchen up to date while blending into the rest of the home's traditional family-friendly style.

"I wanted a room where I could answer homework questions without interrupting meal preparation," said Rocky. She also wanted to be able to work side by side with her spouse without bumping elbows with him or getting hung up by the dishwasher, which couldn't be unloaded when the adjacent cabinet door was open.

With all of this in mind, Kees laid out the kitchen in zones, instead of

Before: Dated, boxy, and inefficient, the old kitchen was arranged poorly and was thus difficult to use. The layout, with its jutting peninsula, could never meet the needs of this family of six.

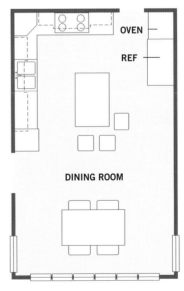

LEFT: Designer Cheryl Kees improved the kitchen's traffic pattern appreciably by widening the entrance to the living room to 10 feet and replacing an underutilized prep area with the refrigerator and oven. A new center island became the kitchen's workhorse.

ABOVE: The floor plan required surprisingly few structural changes. Kees opened up the area by removing a corner prep area and replacing it with a storage wall that holds a bookcase, ovens, and the refrigerator.

finishing touches

ABOVE: For a vent hood like the Parras', this stainless steel Italian-designed chimney unit is widely available.

RIGHT: Finished in mahogany, this 44-inch-tall beech-wood bar stool would make a handsome counter-side seat.

ABOVE: These natural quartz countertops come with antimicrobial protection to inhibit the growth of stain and odor producing bacteria.

TOP TIP
Add storage by clustering tall components, such as a refrigerator and stacked ovens, here framed with a bookcase and cabinets.

hewing to the oft-followed work-triangle approach. The new design would enable several people to complete tasks comfortably and simultaneously, whether they were cooking, eating, or helping a child with homework. For the new cabinets, Kees chose a subtle glaze that added depth to the wood's light stain.

With all of its improvements, the new design called for few structural changes, other than eliminating the soffit and widening the entrance to the living room. Nudging the cooktop over a few inches and repositioning the oven to a spot across the room permitted the use of a dramatic stainless steel hood—a key element in the designer's goal of visually adding height to the 8-foot ceiling.

Gone was the underutilized prep area, situated in the traffic path to the living room and creating an unwanted landing spot for junk. In its place is the "tall corner," as Kees calls it, which draws the eye upward: a counter-depth refrigerator with a bookcase on one side. Across the room, a granite-topped island replaced the peninsula. Its top tier creates an eat-at bar that doubles as a homework center for the Parras' three school-age youngsters.

OPPOSITE: The defined cooktop area features backsplash tile set in a diamond pattern framed by cherry cabinets and a stainless steel hood.

BELOW: Glass-fronted cabinets and the wine storage compartment break up an expanse of cabinet doors. To add headroom over the sink, the plate rack was raised and indented slightly.

BELOW: The honey tones of the new granite countertops and floor tile create a contrast against the richness of the cherry cabinets. Slide-out baskets add storage and a dash of old-world functionality to the kitchen.

what was done

- Installed new cherry cabinets and granite countertops
- Replaced the peninsula with a two-tiered island
- Repositioned the cooktop to accommodate a new exhaust hood
- Upgraded appliances to professional style in stainless steel
- Widened the doorway to the living room to 10 feet
- Improved lighting with strategically placed spotlights

party central

The homeowners are empty nesters more interested in planning parties than preparing pasta, so the 600-square-foot L-shaped kitchen they wanted for their new Westchester County, New York, home was designed accordingly.

"My wife doesn't cook—she makes reservations," the husband explained, laughing. "When we entertain, we have takeout, catered meals, or barbecues, so we didn't really want a kitchen that looked or felt like a kitchen."

ABOVE: The back side of the island sets up a direct channel to the dining area. Angled conveniently toward the main sink, a second oven saves steps in the large kitchen.

To give the space all the elegance of a living room and all the efficiency of a prime food-prep area, Donny Crichton, owner of Merrick Kitchen & Bath, in Merrick, New York, called for classic maple cabinetry that pairs function and flair. "The cabinets resemble luxurious furniture," he said. "Arranging them was like putting together a jigsaw puzzle because every piece of cabinetry had to fit with the coffered ceiling."

The delight is in the details: a monumental arched valance stretches over the sink; a bilevel island sports a hefty butcher block attached at a space-defining dogleg angle; and beaded insets mark the cabinet doors. Grandly integrated into the scheme are the appliances, with a lighted display shelf and cove, complete with curvaceous corbels over the color-coordinated eight-burner range and a set of elaborately paneled doors that conceal a large built-in refrigerator.

"We selected glass-paneled doors for some of the wall cabinets so my wife can display her collection of china and glassware," the husband said.

"The pieces are all in different colors, and, especially when they are illuminated at night, really do set the mood for a party."

The kitchen is positioned as the perfect host space. French doors open onto an Olympic-size swimming pool, and the rest of the space flows into the family room, where guests gather.

A 42-inch flat-screen television, along with two others in the family room, keep the couple informed of current events and provide entertainment for visitors, and a desk at the end of the glass-topped dining table becomes an ideal spot for catching up on correspondence.

When the couple does indulge in some home cooking, the appliances, which include a separate freezer drawer, two dishwashers, and a second oven, are ready and waiting.

"The kitchen is lovely," the husband declared, adding that it so little resembles a place to prepare meals that he rarely calls it by that name. "We feel as though we live in a hotel. But we still have to do our own room service."

OPPOSITE: A spacious kitchen like this one can handle multiple focal points—they break down the experience of the space into individual moments. The main range, set in a carefully composed alcove, is one such spot.

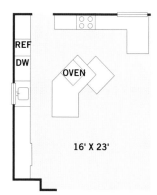

16' X 23'

LEFT: Circulation is free and easy in this kitchen, thanks to the strategic design and placement of the island. Its bent form makes it less formidable or barrier-like than a straight block.

BELOW: The easygoing elegance of this kitchen can be attributed in large part to its guest-friendly floor plan: an open L shape with a dogleg island that subtly divides the space.

BELOW: Luminous onyx counters add a touch of luxe to the kitchen. Their shine is amplified by the simple glossy tile backsplash and enameled sink.

storage with style

Whether a kitchen is designed for one cook or for caterers, storage is a must. Drawers ranging from small apothecary models set into the range hood mantel (below) to extra-deep units for pots and pans, supplanting hinged cabinets, owing to their flexibility and ease of use.

Behind the traditional-style cabinetry, with its fluted pilasters, turned legs, and finger-friendly bin pulls, there are modern storage conveniences. In the unit below, a trio of sliding trays is concealed by a hinged door. Unfettered access to the microwave is achieved by opening two flipper panels, whose doors retract into the sides of the cabinet.

historic expression

Before: Old brick, floral wallpaper, a narrow worktable, and an odd array of appliances, added up to a dark kitchen that could accommodate only one cook at a time. The 13-by-16-foot disjointed layout lacked an eat-in area and adequate lighting. The 1980s decor bore no reference to the Victorian heritage of the home.

Since the early 1990s, the owners of a historic home in the landmarked Montrose section of South Orange, New Jersey, had been restoring their circa-1885 house, room by room. Once they had updated and redone most of the house, they decided to remodel the kitchen, turning for help to designer Sharon L. Sherman, CKD, of Thyme & Place Design, in Wyckoff, New Jersey, and Ulrich, Inc., in Ridgewood. Without moving walls, Sherman opened up the space, and also had vintage-look cabinets and new appliances put in place.

The house had an abundance of Victorian wood trim throughout, so Sherman decided to add bead board to the new painted-maple cabinets. She also augmented the recessed ceiling lights with antique chandeliers. A limestone top was chosen for the island as a way to create contrast with the slate on nearby countertops.

OPPOSITE: Designer Sharon Sherman worked within the existing space, placing a new cooktop and built-in exhaust system where a range once stood. The angled wall backs an existing fireplace chimney. Sherman matched that angle in positioning the panel-covered refrigerator. The freestanding cherry island contains a drawer-style refrigerator and an undermount sink on one side, stools for sit-down snacks on the other.

RIGHT: A breakfast table and chairs back up to the banquette window seat. Restored wood flooring flows into tiles, set like bricks, in the hall leading to a laundry room and porch.

what was done

- Retained the old wood flooring and wood trim and added new woodwork in the style of the original
- Removed the lowered ceiling, which added a foot of unused vertical space
- Moved a door leading to the front parlor to make room for the refrigerator
- Custom-designed a baking counter for her (she's 5 foot 2) that is 4 inches lower than the rest of the counters
- Created an island with a limestone top that can function as both a work space for preparing food as well as a sit-down area for dining

design magic

Fashionably furnished and comfortable—these are among the qualities most homeowners would like their ideal kitchen to embody. It's not an easy balance to strike, but when done right the results are impressive. An outstanding example: the cooking and eating spaces in Donna and Ross Roberts' Michigan home in an area near Lake Michigan. It was chiefly Donna who worked this magic in layout and design along with Elizabeth Firebaugh, CKD, of Signature Kitchens, in Petosky.

"I wanted the kitchen to have an old-world flair that would be quite traditional," Donna said. "But it had to be architectural, not frilly or Country French." The cherry paneling and cherry floor, both stained burnt umber, coordinate with wood in the adjoining breakfast and sitting rooms. "I like the dark tones of the cabinet wood as well as the gold accents of the chandeliers and chair fabrics," Donna declared. "We worked hard on getting a shade that didn't have a heavy library look," Firebaugh added. "We struggled over this, staining large sample areas."

Many features of the floor plan were determined with cooking and company in mind. Granite counters seemed the ideal surface for Donna's many culinary projects—like pasta making. The large central island often seats grandchildren, while the breakfast room easily accommodates six diners—enabling guests to gather and Donna to remain part of the scene while she cooks. Another sink next to two dishwashers gives maximum efficiency to the chef, while a bar sink in the island is allotted to Ross if he wants to help. "I'm very stingy with my sink!" said Donna. A wide pathway separates the refrigerator and double ovens from the island, keeping everyone safe from kitchen casualties. "You can't open a hot oven if you're banging into someone's back when you do," Donna explained.

Professional-quality appliances and storage are found throughout the kitchen. Donna, a gas-burner cook, included electric hobs on her cooktop so that her daughters, when visiting, can cook with the electricity they prefer. A warming drawer under the dual ovens gets used for frequent dinner guests, and a microwave has its own alcove right by the refrigerator, so

OPPOSITE: Closing off a former stairway in the corner of the kitchen helped Donna gain more counter and storage space. It also helped improve the flow of foot traffic in the kitchen.

vintage-style plumbing

In kitchen design as in fashion, it's the little details that make the biggest splash. Putting a shiny, streamlined faucet in a formal, traditional kitchen is like donning a baseball cap when wearing a ball gown. Instead, consider vintage styles with old-time finishes such as antique brass, copper, or satin nickel. Any of these would help perpetuate the illusion that your faucet has been around a while.

ABOVE: No doubt about it, copper is the essence of period style. The traditional shape of this faucet, in a copper finish, effectively camouflages the modern convenience of a pullout spray. The faucet is at home with other copper accessories.

TOP: A pump-style faucet with an oiled bronze finish adds an informal accent to this otherwise formal kitchen. Available as either a single-lever model or a two-handle version (a matching vegetable spray is optional), it is as functional as it is fit.

BELOW: The sink end of the island is visible from down the hall at the front door. The designer planned this custom-carved bow front to make a more elegant, less utilitarian statement to people entering the home.

BOTTOM: Fluted cherry columns give the dining island the look of a formal table. The rounded wood and granite ends of the island echo the arches of the kitchen door and the cooktop's brick alcove.

BELOW: The exhaust hood's recessed light projects onto the professional-style cooktop, which includes a grill, gas and electric burners, and a deep fryer—all of which get a hefty workout when the family hosts dinner gatherings.

BOTTOM: Carved wood corbels give a glass-fronted upper cabinet a special touch. Its furniture-like appearance is what makes the cabinet such an attention-getter, according to designer Elizabeth Firebaugh.

14'6" X 14'6"

LEFT: Closing off a former stairway in the corner of the kitchen set the stage for creating more counter and storage space, and also helped step up control of foot traffic.

RIGHT: Pairing a gooseneck faucet and filtered-water dispenser ensured totally efficient pot filling in the undermount sink. The cooktop is located nearby, making the trip from basin to burner a short, easy commute for the cook.

the children can spread their snacks out conveniently. A custom spice drawer hard by the cooktop aligns fifty seasonings in alphabetical order, and two upper cabinets have glass and open fronts to lighten the look of the room.

Perhaps most notably, the hearth-like stone alcove that frames the cooktop needed a deft touch to marry its bulk to the granite and tile materials in the two abutting surfaces. "At first, we were going to sheathe the exhaust hood in stone," said Firebaugh. "But that seemed too cumbersome, so we altered our plan and opted for wood. For the same reason—a need for lightness—we also decided not to have a stone backsplash." (The duo eventually chose a classical tile mural—highly decorative but practical in its low maintenance.) They even agonized over what material should show in the small triangular recesses behind the sloping sides of the hood. The decision: a touch more stone. "These small slices of stone bolster the illusion that this alcove really is built into an old existing chimney," Firebaugh said "It's these small details that often make such a difference."

RIGHT: A near-panoramic view embraces the breakfast area. Formal details, such as the chandelier and pelmet, are softened by the laid-back beauty of abundant foliage.

reclaiming the past

When Lily Kanter and her husband, Marc Sarosi, bought their historic Mill Valley, California, home, the clock was already ticking. Lily was four months pregnant with their third child, and their circa-1907 plantation-style house was not exactly in move-in condition.

Built by Bernard Maybeck, a legendary Bay Area architect of the time, the three-story house was among the first designed there to withstand earthquakes. So while its good bones remained intact, its interiors needed work—especially the kitchen. "It looked like it hadn't been touched since the forties," Lily recalled. "And it was pink!" A gut job was in order.

Enter designer Tineke Triggs, founder of the San Francisco firm Artistic Designs for Living, whose task was to restore the kitchen's period elegance while adding modern upgrades and creating a space ample and comfortable enough for a growing family—all within a tight time frame.

Fortunately, the homeowners and their designer didn't have far to go for

their design muse. "Lily loved a bank of floor-to-ceiling cabinets that remained from the original kitchen," Triggs reported. With its recessed-panel doors and vintage surface-mount catches, the pantry had great presence and character. "We replaced the hinges and put in new glazing," Triggs added, "and this became our inspiration."

Period styling seamlessly punctuates the space, from the generous apron-front sink to the divided-light doors on upper cabinets and cup bin pulls on lower cabinetry. Tile treatments reflect a bygone era, but with a twist: a classic subway tile backsplash looks fresh in celadon; low-maintenance slate covers the floor, bordered with a classic hexagonal tile. But this kitchen also has a family-friendly point of view. Triggs removed the wall between the kitchen and mudroom to create a dining area, and Lily added three stools to the dark-walnut island to accommodate her young brood.

While most of the kitchen's individual features are stylish, interesting, or both, one stands out

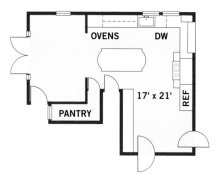

ABOVE: The kitchen was upsized when one of the walls was removed. This made way for a separate eating area, while an adjacent pantry holds overflow storage. A beefy island claims almost 25 square feet of storage and work space.

as unique: the view of San Francisco Triggs brought into the kitchen. Because the view is actually from the dining room, Triggs added a pair of windows to the left of the range (and below a set of cabinets) that look through the dining room to capture the vista. But perhaps the most impressive aspect of the renovation was finishing not only on time but early, with a few weeks to spare. "We began the remodel February 15," Lily recalled, "and we moved in June 15—barely two weeks before our third son arrived." By then the vintage kitchen was set to serve its modern family.

OPPOSITE: The kitchen's bead-board ceiling was left untouched for an authentic patina. The pair of brass-and-glass pendants suspended over the island are knockoffs of the period's lighting.

RIGHT: Designed for modern living, the new kitchen has plenty of storage—enough dishes to serve fifty!— and an island just right for casual meals. But materials, such as marble and bead board, pay homage to the home's 1907 heritage. The cabinet on the left is original.

BELOW: A cutting board set into the marble countertop creates a mini prep area, a location that is convenient to the adjacent sink.

BOTTOM: Looking down is a feast for the eyes: popular in the past, white hex tiles border a slate floor laid in a running bond pattern. Base cabinets are finished with furniture-like feet.

BELOW: A dedicated cooking zone was crafted by placing the range in an alcove, where it has the look of an old-fashioned hearth. Within the alcove, a shallow cabinet keeps spices handy.

double duty

Sometimes the quest for places to put things results in an avalanche of cabinets that make kitchens look monolithic and boxy. A tasteful armoire adds aesthetic variation without sacrificing storage. Armoires can serve a variety of functions, from storing staples to housing appliances. While their uses are diverse, armoires heavily favor traditional styling. And they readily lend themselves to personalizing—they can be assembled using standard components available from any cabinet manufacturer.

Typical units consist of an upper cabinet sitting directly on a countertop, with another cabinet below. Drawers can be added to hold flat items and moderate the proportions of the piece. Then come decorative elements: molding, appliqués, and side panels that, all together, create a cohesive look. Even minor touches like knobs and pulls can greatly enhance the impact of this workhorse unit. After all, the cosmetic appeal of an armoire is just as vital as its practical benefit.

A splendid built-in china hutch

BELOW: This custom unit contrasts an upper portion divided in thirds and a lower portion split in two. The glass doors add to the illusion of open shelves. Below are shorter cabinets with solid doors. Directly under the counter are four drawers and a valance toekick. Set into a nook, the unit requires no side panels, but it does include understated molding on top.

The perfect chef's armoire

TOP, RIGHT: Beneath the decorative crown molding is a 15-inch-deep cabinet with Prairie-style glass doors on top of a spice-drawer unit. Molding separating upper cabinets and counter is repeated under the bottom cabinet, a 31½-inch-wide double-door wall unit with vanity legs.

A morning pick-me-up station

BOTTOM, RIGHT: Although sold as a single unit, this armoire's distinct storage zones are unmistakable. Between the glass-door upper and solid-door lower areas is a ledge for serving coffee or juice. The fold-down door provides a light-duty landing area and hides the appliances when breakfast is over. A row of drawers completes the storage. Side and toe panels tie it all together, and a crown molding caps it off.

country charmers

Country style involves choice, not geography, for it is equally possible to have a country kitchen in an urban high-rise as in a house in the woods. Think of natural materials: wood, brick, and stone. Then add baskets, homespun rugs, tin ornaments, colorful pottery, and handpainted tiles. Shelves of spices, bins of vegetables, hanging cups and cookware—all add color and texture to the informal mix. A country kitchen may look unplanned, but in the best examples every inch serves the cook and the household.

the perfect mix

At first glance, the kitchen in John and Joanne Manacek's 1990s colonial-style home appeared adequate. After all, it boasted an island for dining and prep, decent appliances, a pantry, and a separate eating space. But looks are deceiving, according to designers Karen Sciascia and Martha Gargano, of A Matter of Style, in Cheshire, Connecticut. "Lack of organized storage and narrow aisles made working there difficult," said Gargano, especially when the couple entertained.

To open up the kitchen's work area, Sciascia and Gargano removed the obtrusive island. They relocated eating areas to a new peninsula counter and to a cozy 100-square-foot addition, which extends out from the old dining space.

The new room has windows on three sides and a built-in banquette; the former eating area is now a pathway that directs traffic past the main work space. The kitchen itself was outfitted with white-painted cabinets with a charcoal glaze, cherry floors, and granite counters. Bead-board siding adds interest to the banquette, peninsula, and pantry doors.

"Joanne's big concern was organization," said Gargano. To address this, the designers installed a built-in wine rack, roll-out drawers for utensils, a spice drawer by the range, and drawer dividers for trays and cutlery. One of John's favorite amenities is the appliance garage. "It stores the blender, the toaster—everything he needs to prepare breakfast," said Sciascia.

Before: The location of the old island created narrow aisles, which made for crowded working conditions. Cabinets were plain and serviceable but lacked customized storage. Laminate counters gave the room a drab appearance.

OPPOSITE: The counter was designed to angle outward, opening up the work area and at the same time providing additional dining space. Along with double crown molding and arched details, the space includes a bumped-out window with a granite sill over the sink, an area used for growing herbs and displaying topiary.

what was done

- Built a new dining space onto the kitchen, adding 100 square feet
- Removed the island and created new eating and food-prep areas
- Installed granite counters with ogee edges
- Built in customized storage to accommodate dishes and utensils
- Put in new appliances, including a glass cooktop, double ovens, and a built-in refrigerator
- Upgraded task and overhead lighting

Before

LEFT: The narrow counter next to the refrigerator became a catch-all for paper clutter. An oversize chandelier made the ceiling appear very low.

After

BELOW: Double ovens, one of Manacek's requests, reside where a pantry once stood; a new three-door pantry compensates for lost storage. Above the pantry, glass-paned doors reveal display space for pretty dishes.

RIGHT: Cherry floors complement the kitchen's white cabinets, which provide an abundance of storage in the new space.

BELOW: The new dining nook features a bumped-out window wall overlooking the Connecticut woodlands. A buffet at right serves as a decorative link between the two spaces. The wall sconces above it add a slightly formal note.

with southern gusto

"Recreating meals that our ancestors prepared, while weaving in convenience products that were unavailable in their time but are accessible to today's home cooks." This is the ambitious goal of cookbook author and Food Network star Paula Deen. Acknowledging Deen's respect for traditional amenities and her keen preference for a family-friendly space–"where everyone has a seat"– interior designer Ingrid Leess created a heart-of-the-home kitchen efficient enough to appeal as much to a skilled home cook as to an experienced chef.

Honoring Deen's requests, designer Leess made sure the kitchen included a cooktop, a wall oven mounted under-counter, two dishwashers, raised wine storage, and a refrigerator/freezer, plus additional refrigerator and freezer drawers. Completing the second of the three cooking stations, a microwave, warming drawer, and second wall oven are contained in a single built-in unit.

Two cabinet styles and finishes dominate, with a third tone introduced to accent the dining side of the island and the high-backed utility bench. Work surfaces are quartz, and two tones of quartz top the counters on both sides of the island. All surfaces have double-ogee edging.

Flooring here is natural hardwood, with ceramic tiles inset on the dining side of the island. A chandelier that recalls traditional design makes the work and eating areas of the island feel separate and special. Recessed and under-cabinet lighting is linked to a timed dimmer system that enables the cook to predetermine where and when the lights should be focused.

Cabinet details enhance the room, with corbels, V-groove paneling, rope-patterned trim elements, and onlays with a woven look that provide strong visual enrichment. Classic crown molding, decorative shelving, and slide-out baskets for vegetable storage complete the country look.

In addition, the kitchen contains space for Deen's extensive cookbook library and for displaying important serving pieces and collectibles. Hidden assets in the cabinetry include space-saving corner storage units, deep drawers for pots and pans, pullout pantry units, and a pop-up shelf for a blender or food processor.

The centerpiece of the kitchen is clearly the 60-inch exhaust-hood ensemble, which features open storage plus spice shelving and tiered storage

OPPOSITE: A rustic terra-cotta tile insert in the hardwood-plank floor defines a separate setting for the two-sided island with a raised divider. A bronze-finish chandelier sheds a romantic glow on diners and also adds ambient light for anyone working on the food-prep side.

LEFT: A copper-toned food processor rises to near counter height on a spring-loaded pop-up shelf. When the appliance is no longer needed, it and the shelf can be pressed back down and tucked into a base cabinet.

BELOW: Quartz in two finishes tops the divided dine-and-work island, with its bronze-finished undermount bar sink. The brushed bronze single-handled faucet has a pullout spray.

ABOVE: A refrigerator with two freezer drawers is installed beside a glass-fronted wine cooler and drawer-style refrigerator/freezer combo. To the left, atop slide-out vegetable baskets, a quartz counter backed by Italian mosaic tile creates an auxiliary work space.

design tips

- Three different finishes point up the design of kitchen cabinetry as furniture; each unit is set off with shapely architectural details.

- A two-level island defines food-prep and dining areas, and also ensures a subtle separation between cook and kibitzers.

- Display areas and open shelving help make the kitchen a showcase of personal expression.

- Angled corners reduce dead storage space and increase cooking gear accessibility.

- Wallpaper, paint, and window decoration extend a palette that spans the rich wood cabinet tones and the orange-red sink.

- Italian ceramic-tile backsplash in earth tones is functional and decorative, providing cool contrast to the overall warmth of the room.

BELOW: A gas cooktop is mounted above an undercounter wall oven. Designer Leess selected 2½-by-2½-inch Italian tiles in six colors to create a backsplash that rises up to a built-in exhaust hood. Another drawer-style refrigerator/freezer plus a second dishwasher make the adjacent island a complete workstation.

RIGHT: An appliance wall—equipped with an oven, microwave, and warming drawer—provides a niche for a bead-board-backed bench in a contrasting tone and finish. Crown molding enhances the architecture of these highly detailed hardwood cabinets.

behind closed doors. Another effective concealment: the division between the island's cooking and eating areas, which would enable a cook to serve informally and also ensure that no diner would ever see a sink or counter cluttered with dishes.

This kitchen was designed as a showcase for the skills of a professional chef, but also as a place where family and friends will always feel welcome.

timeless country flair

Before: Cooktop, wall ovens, microwave, and refrigerator were crammed into one end of the room. In the remodel, the window was moved and only the new refrigerator and microwave were placed close to where the old ones stood.

Limited work surfaces, an inefficient layout, appliances that no longer worked properly—these were the flaws Gina Waymire had to deal with in the kitchen of the fifty-year-old home she and her husband, Chris Jerome, bought in Albuquerque, New Mexico. Waymire recalled that it took a year to develop a remodeling plan that addressed all her concerns.

"I spend a lot of time in my kitchen," she explained, "and our old one was completely nonfunctional." Once she knew what she wanted, she turned to Tim Rizek Jr., of Rizek Custom Homes & Remodeling, in Albuquerque, who agreed to tackle the project. His first chore was to gut the 14½-by-17-foot space, removing old cabinets, appliances, and flooring. "Gina wanted the sink in the center of the outside wall," he recalled. "She also wanted a large window centered over it." Old corner windows were eliminated in favor of a new triple window, and Rizek added an 8-inch bump-out to give the window more prominence while adding depth to the counter. The doorway

linking the kitchen and dining room became an arch that matched the opening between the dining room and hall. Waymire requested wood flooring, which, along with the white-painted cabinets and reproduction light fixtures, would give the kitchen a vintage look. But before the new quarter-sawn white oak strips could be installed, the old tile floor had to be removed along with four layers of linoleum and rotted-out subflooring. The new floor was selected to match wood in the rest of the house.

Waymire spent the most time choosing the trim tile that extends between rows of white subway tile around the window and behind the range. She and her husband had salvaged pieces of original art deco-style tile from a kitchen remodeling in their previous home. "We wanted to copy the look we had," she said. "I spent hours on the phone and the Internet until I found a tile company that had just started producing this exact tile design. The timing was perfect."

Although planning her kitchen was not a full-time job, Waymire said it did become a demanding hobby: "I don't think there's anything else here that I feel so comfortable with."

OPPOSITE: Homeowner Waymire said that once she decided that the sink should be centered under a new window on the outside wall, it was obvious where her new dual-fuel range and butcher-block-topped island should be placed.

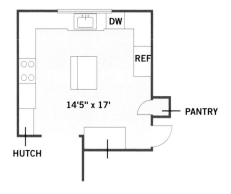

ABOVE: The new kitchen occupies the same space as the old one. The difference is how the elements are arranged, the scale and location of the window, and the size and placement of the doorway leading into the dining room. The homeowner said that by adding the island and hutch-like cabinets to the wall adjacent to the archway, she was able to expand her kitchen's storage and work spaces by 20 percent.

BELOW: The doorway was moved and expanded into an open arch to make room for storage cabinets and work space on an adjacent wall.

Before

BELOW, CENTER: A narrow doorway on the far wall connected the kitchen and dining room.

BELOW, RIGHT: Seen from the dining room, the small doorway that opened into the kitchen became a tight fit when serving meals. The contractor moved and expanded that doorway, echoing the arched opening from the entry hall.

After

OPPOSITE: Bin-style hardware and vintage-style pendants add country touches to a cutting-edge space. Waymire says she likes to spread open her cookbooks on the island, and her two children enjoy doing homework there. "There's more space on this side of the island," she said.

BELOW: An elegant satin-finish nickel faucet with lever handle is mounted above a stainless steel undermount double sink. By creating an 8-inch extension for the new window behind the sink, Rizek could add work space to the counter area.

what was done

- Replaced cabinets, counters, and appliances
- Created soffits so that new wall cabinets would appear to rise to the ceiling
- Blocked off the corner windows and centered a new window in the exterior wall
- Expanded the kitchen, dining room doorway into a 48-inch archway
- Put down new wood flooring
- Installed a butcher-block-topped island
- Added recessed ceiling lights and pendant fixtures

a style-savvy update

Before

ABOVE: With worn vinyl flooring, inadequate cabinets, fake butcher-block counters, and dated wallpaper, the kitchen—last remodeled in the 1970s—was out of sync with the rest of the 1913 house. A shortage of counters and lack of cabinets created a dysfunctional work area. An adjoining unheated entryway and cluttered mudroom added a claustrophobic feeling.

what was done

- Removed a door between kitchen and mudroom
- Installed a new heated pantry that includes a new window, gardening center, and storage cabinets
- Eliminated an old pantry to make room for the new refrigerator and provide space for a powder room
- Built custom cabinets on site to match the original early-1900 style of the home
- Added upper cabinets for increased storage
- Installed a hutch to add storage and provide another serving space adjacent to the dining room

When a Portland, Oregon, couple wanted the kitchen of their ninety-year-old house restored to its roots, they turned to Andrew Curtis, of Full Circa Vintage Remodelers, in Portland. Curtis, who earned a master's degree in historic preservation, worked with the family long distance while they were living abroad. "The homeowners wanted a renovation in keeping with the style of their 1913 home, which has many Craftsman details," he remarked. "They also like to cook, so the kitchen had to function efficiently."

For looks, period-accurate custom cabinets with cup handles, new crown molding, and maroon-and-tan vinyl floor tiles give the room authentic appeal. Two upper cabinets, constructed without doors, and backsplashes made of rectangular subway tiles lend bonus effects.

For function, high-end appliances and granite counters enable the family to prepare meals comfortably. "The homeowners were adamant about having no undercabinet or canned lights," said Curtis. The kitchen thus relies on sunlight plus four ceiling fixtures— reproductions of classic schoolhouse lights—for its new sparkle.

French accented

Designer Mari Dolby usually spends the bulk of her day poring over fabrics and fixtures, furniture and floor coverings looking for inspiration to create beautiful rooms for her clients. So when she started planning the kitchen of her own home—a seventy-year-old farmhouse on land just outside Philadelphia formerly deeded to William Penn—it was a fabric swatch and a piece of French crockery emblazoned with a bird of paradise that sparked the design process.

"I love the look and feel of an authentic French country kitchen," said Dolby, who shares the home with her husband, Kent, and two teenage sons. "I wanted my kitchen to be warm and cozy and look as if it had been there forever."

Instead of reworking the original circa-1960s kitchen, Dolby absorbed the dining room, netting an additional 150 square feet. But the exchange proved tricky since there were fewer interior walls for cabinets. According to kitchen designer Julie Ann Stoner, CKD, who collaborated on the project,

LEFT: The hand-hewn fir beams, tumbled limestone counters, and slate floor of the 20-by-20-foot space come together to create an appealingly eclectic French country look.

"the biggest consideration was that as Mari is an avid entertainer, we had to make sure we had enough storage for all her serving pieces and equipment." She also explained that Dolby preferred using large furniture pieces instead of relying on wall-mounted cabinetry.

Except for the range, which sits in a brick-lined alcove resembling an old-fashioned hearth, all of the commercial appliances are housed in handcrafted, one-of-a-kind cabinet units that are virtually indistinguishable from the authentic antique pieces Dolby often brings home from her travels to France. She explained that "the range is the only readily identifiable appliance in the kitchen. You have to look really hard to find the rest." This is especially true of the refrigerator, housed in a custom-built breakfront cleverly fitted with false-bottom drawers that mimic the lines of an early 1800s cupboard.

Mari was equally fearless about mixing colors and finishes. "I actually started with the variegated slate floor and pulled all the warm muted colors from it," she said. Cotswald green graces the legs of the pastry table; Prussian blue turns up on the cupboard, designed to stow

BELOW, LEFT: Incorporating the former dining room into the new floor plan added 150 square feet to the kitchen. With wall space at a premium, much of this extra area would be filled by several freestanding furniture-like storage units.

BELOW, RIGHT: A large armoire takes full advantage of the kitchen's limited wall space.

BOTTOM, LEFT: The apron sink is extra deep to accommodate Dolby's pasta pot. Lattice patterned doors, turned legs, and furniture-style feet evoke a cottage-like feel.

BOTTOM, RIGHT: In a setting designed to look like one of Dolby's antique discoveries, the top portion of this custom-built cupboard contains a pair of side-by-side refrigerators. Integrated panels conceal the open freezer drawers. Canned goods are stored in a narrow pull-out pantry sandwiched in between.

OPPOSITE: A brick-tiled alcove housing a 48-inch-wide professional-style range is the kitchen's focal point. Niches on either side hold cooking oils and condiments. The backsplash features a large handpainted English tile.

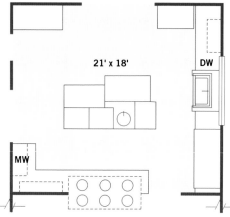

coffee supplies; pale yellow brightens lattice paneling applied below the sink.

An L-shaped island, equipped with a raised maple butcher block, marble-topped roll-out pastry table, and ample limestone counters, further illustrates Dolby's "mix don't match" theory. As she pointed out, "It has three different surfaces, yet nothing competes—everything goes together wonderfully."

For this enlightened Francophile, it's all in the mix. "I think French design is timeless," Dolby declared. "It will never go out of style."

cozy context with grandeur

OPPOSITE: A sweeping wall-wide arch gives visual impact to a relatively small kitchen.

RIGHT: Concealing small, modern appliances helps preserve the room's old-time atmosphere.

CENTER, RIGHT: Combining time-tested materials in unexpected ways keeps the kitchen classic and fresh.

BOTTOM, RIGHT: Rollout shelves in the base cabinets make it considerably easier to store and access heavy cookware.

As it is rare for a kitchen to age gracefully, a great many homeowners face a thorny dilemma: how to create a modern work area without violating visual harmony within the original house. This design for a new kitchen in a 1920s English-style home meets the challenge with elegant efficiency.

Working within the confines of the existing 11½-by-10½-foot room, Cyndy Cantley, CKD, of Birmingham, Alabama, arranged two parallel counters that would fit seamlessly with existing architectural features—a dramatic archway entrance at one end and a divided-light glass service door and window on the opposite wall. With classic symmetry in mind, she created an efficient design on an intimate scale.

The client wanted her new kitchen to respond to the stylistic integrity of the house. As a first step to achieving this goal, Cantley chose natural materials in contrasting finishes: white-painted base cabinetry and stained cypress for the hanging cabinets, and counters of Indiana limestone.

"I wanted the distressed-cypress wall cabinets to appear like found pieces of furniture delivered to this kitchen," the designer explained. "The varying finish choices also add interest to the room and avoid the often mundane look of wall-to-wall cabinetry."

A similar approach also influenced the choice of wall and floor finishes. A custom stucco topcoat applied by a local artist brought textural nuance to the entry arch and walls, and the warm yellow color of the end wall accentuates the natural look of the hardwood floor and cypress cabinetry.

Blending features and finishes identified with specific eras takes creativity and verve; attempts lacking a sure hand often end up a confused jumble. But creating just the right eclectic look is permanently rewarding—the design bridges eras in a way a fashion-driven "statement" cannot. "We strive to create efficient kitchens which are also timeless," said Cantley. "Moreover, we enjoy mixing traditional elements."

There is a special pleasure in tracing the various influences behind Cantley's choices for this kitchen. The glass-door cupboards flanking the new sink echo a traditional kitchen of the early 1900s, as do the white subway tiles of the backsplash. Although atypical of a 1920s kitchen—in those days, linoleum floors were de rigueur—the polished

BELOW: Cool stainless steel has become a timeless neutral tone in kitchens of all styles, contrasting effectively with both painted and natural surfaces. Glass-fronted cupboards lighten the look of the cabinetry while echoing window design in the room.

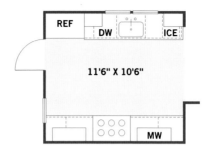

LEFT: In a kitchen like this, with only two "working" walls and neither an island nor a peninsula, uninterrupted stretches of counters become critical elements.

hardwood flooring picks up on the wood floors in other rooms.

In a modest-size kitchen like this one, fitting in modern appliances without sacrificing storage can be a struggle. Although it may be tempting to overdo it by overloading a space, simplicity trumps congestion every time. For example, for both spatial and stylistic reasons, an island simply would not fit here. To optimize storage and working areas, Cantley placed the dishwasher and ice maker on either side of the sink, and centered an imposing 40-inch-wide French range on the opposing wall, leaving straight runs of clear counter space on either side.

With the microwave tucked into one of the upper cabinets, counters are kept free; pull-out shelving in the base cabinet units allows easy access to cookware. The stainless steel exhaust hood is another sophisticated design element; although contemporary in material, the exposed flue echoes the look and feel of the 1920s.

Simplicity in layout, timelessness in materials, efficiency in planning—these design fundamentals work together to maximize the potential of this warmly intimate space.

small-kitchen smarts

The vision thing: It may be natural to focus on maximizing counter space and storage in a small kitchen, but devote some of your budget and efforts to features, textures, and colors that add visual zing to the finished room. In this kitchen, designer Cyndy Cantley employed contrasting cabinet finishes and surfacing materials; a local artisan's custom stucco wall finish added textural interest.

At home with nature: Using a variety of natural materials ensures a degree of design timelessness. Remember the fad for gray-and-white kitchens in the 1980s? Dull, dull, dull. Part of that era's charmless look stemmed from its reliance on plastic finishes and bland, boxlike cabinetry. This kitchen's varied palette of natural materials—honed limestone counters, glazed ceramic tile backsplash, and rich wood flooring and cabinetry—lends the small space unmistakable elegance.

Let there be light: And make sure there is plenty of it—natural if possible, artificial if not. Lighting can make an extraordinary difference in a small kitchen. This one enjoys an abundance of daylight from two windows and a divided-light glass door. If you must deal with a dark kitchen, consider enlarging a window or adding a glass door or skylight. Address task lighting with undercabinet or track-light fixtures, and boost reflectivity with glossy paint or shiny tile in pale or bright tones.

farmhouse fancies

Farmhouse design is as much about the way a kitchen feels as the way it looks. A farmhouse kitchen can be many things; what it cannot be is rigid and formal. Most of all, it's earthy. Painted cabinets, a time-worn kitchen table, and a stone or wood-plank floor make a visual statement. Often, a crackling fire plus the smell of fresh-baked bread and drying herbs add to the ambience. There is also the iconic farmhouse sink, with its apron front and unique profile. Think of a kitchen you could stride into and not stop to remove muddy boots. That is true farmhouse informality.

a really smart solution

RIGHT: With just one small window stuck off in a corner, the old kitchen was usually a dark, gloomy place. Now the whole wall has windows.

OPPOSITE: As in many kitchen remodels, adding an island saves energy— in this case, the cook's. Jamie and Anne Orvis chose a green base for their island to break up the expanse of white cabinets.

They are good for the planet, for peace of mind, and also for the wallet. The latest energy-conscious products are also just plain good. This entire kitchen is equipped with appliances, lighting, and other products that have been given the Energy Star label. (A U.S. government program, Energy Star certifies each year an array of products that meet strict energy-efficiency guidelines in their respective categories.)

With advice from home-improvement experts and help from the Environmental Protection Agency, which administers Energy Star, a dated kitchen morphed into an energy-efficient space for a young family residing in the Northeast. Jamie and Anne Orvis live in a twenty-five-year-old Colonial in Fairfield, Connecticut, with their kids—Ryan and Amanda—and their dog, Maui. Although they don't consider themselves hard-core environmentalists, they are loyal recyclers with a concern for the environment. "We only have one earth," Jamie said.

To accomplish the remodel, Jamie hired architect Rob Sanders, of Wilton, Connecticut, to map out the structural and engineering details. The Orvises wanted to expand their diminutive kitchen—and upgrade their small, inefficient appliances—but did not want to increase the amount of energy they used or the expense of using it. They took their ideas to Lowe's in Orange, Connecticut, to work with kitchen specialist Fozia Rafique. "She was tremendous," Jamie declared. "We went up there with a floor plan and said, 'Here's the space. We want an island with bar stools, lots of storage, and an area for a desk.'"

According to Rafique, it was the planning up front that helped the project go smoothly. "I was careful to ask Anne and Jamie exactly what they wanted and where they wanted it," she said. Rafique collected some samples, showed the Orvises various kitchen cabinet styles and colors, plus available surfaces, then guided them through the selection of energy-saving appliances. "Working with a home center made the design process so much easier since everything we needed for the new kitchen was right there in the store," Jamie recalled.

The home now boasts an array of new Energy Star-rated appliances, including a dishwasher, refrigerator, dehumidifier, and washing machine,

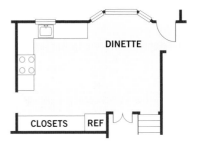

Before: Despite being an open kitchen, the skimpy size, lack of storage, and dearth of windows made it a challenging space to work in.

After: The new addition not only expanded the room but also provided more storage and countertop work space. The appliances and island are placed in one area, making it an ideal layout for cooking and entertaining.

BELOW: Because Jamie Orvis loves to cook, the 48-inch cooktop has been a welcome addition. The coordinated exhaust hood removes enough air to eliminate the fumes and odors produced by the large, powerful cooking surface below.

energy star gazing

The U.S. Environmental Protection Agency initiated the Energy Star program back in 1992 to help commercial users and residential consumers protect the environment through energy efficiency.

The Energy Star label goes on products that are in the top 25 percent in their category in terms of energy efficiency. Technology has evolved to the point where you can now purchase more powerful appliances that save a substantial amount of energy over older models. Energy Star units are not only less expensive to operate; they also tend to be technically superior.

RIGHT: The old, small kitchen was made to feel even more cramped by the tiny table that was placed there for performing food-prep tasks.

BELOW, RIGHT: The new island adds work space, has room for a large sink, and can accommodate three diners. Thanks to the room's additional square footage, the kitchen table can now sit in an open space flooded with light.

plus Energy Star lighting, to go along with energy-saving windows, thermostat, and a water heater Jamie installed earlier.

For this project, they were looking at just one room, but there's so much more you can do throughout a home. This one room started saving energy for the Orvises right away, however. Although the new kitchen is nearly double the size of the old one, it actually functions on less energy than the old one did.

Not surprisingly, all the new appliances perform much better too. "The dishwasher can work with heated drying or not," said Anne. "I often try

what was done

- Expanded the kitchen from 122 square feet to 250 square feet
- Replaced old appliances with new Energy Star-rated units
- Installed a center island
- Removed a small window and replaced it with a wall of windows
- Added a walk-in pantry
- Replaced vinyl flooring with hardwood
- Added a workhorse desk area

storage innovations

After meal-end cleanup, the Orvises can pop wet sponges into a tilt-out bin below the sink to let them dry—and keep bacteria at bay. This bonus storage eases counter clutter and puts an otherwise unused space to work.

Pull-out drawers keep Anne's spice jars aligned and visible. Just as important as their organization is the convenient placement. They are right in the prep zone, beside the cooktop, where Anne usually needs them.

not to do the heated-dry to save energy, and it works out fine."

Vargas pointed out that this is important when considering Energy Star-rated products, emphasizing that "You get the same technical ability, but you get it with less energy." In the Orvises' kitchen the refrigerator is a prime example. As Jamie pointed out, "one of the more welcome features of the new kitchen is the fact that the refrigerator motor does not have to run all the time."

As they subtracted energy costs while planning their kitchen update, the Orvises also added smart design. A key addition was the pantry, a walk-in space beside the refrigerator that claimed real estate from the old living room. Anne also appreciated the new center island, not only for its visual impact, but also for its convenience—providing bonus work space as well as a sizable sink carved into the surface—and the fact that she can be working there and still chat with anyone seated at the dining table. Anne and Jamie ultimately found themselves spending more time cooking because being in their kitchen was so enjoyable.

budget barn revival

The converted barn in Essex, Connecticut, that Suzanne and Bob O'Brien bought as a weekend home was modern with a traditional farmhouse feel, except for its small 1970s kitchen. There, clumsy, oversize appliances and cookie-cutter cabinets were at variance with the rustic style in the rest of the house.

Seeking an open, family-friendly kitchen, the couple asked Beth Veillette, a custom-kitchen designer at Hanford Cabinet & Woodworking, in Old Saybrook, to help transform the space with color and a stylish farmhouse decor.

Budget constraints forced Veillette to work around obstacles too costly to change, such as the terra-cotta tile floor, set in concrete, that covered the house's entire first floor. She chose to complement the tiles with Shaker-style cabinets in the same color as the original barn door, which remains in place in the dining room.

To offset and balance the dominant red tone, granite countertops in a crisp black-and-white pattern, white bead board wall panels, and an old-fashioned cast-iron sink were added.

Another restriction was an 18-inch-high exterior stone wall inset with three windows and baseboard heaters, which would have been prohibitively expensive to bump out in an effort to expand the space. So, to highlight the existing windows, Veillette installed custom cabinets over a buffet designed with legs to create enough space for baseboard heating and also to protect the cabinets from the heat. The buffet is designed with an antique distressed-pine countertop to match the ceiling's original beams, which were left exposed.

To provide more storage and display space, Veillette added a glass-fronted cabinet above the sink. "I love the openness of the kitchen," Suzanne exulted, when the work was finally done. "I'm so pleased that it's not wall-to-wall cabinetry."

Minimizing the impact of the appliances was another consideration for this farmhouse-style space. Identical barn-like paneling conceals the new 27-inch-wide side-by-side refrigerator, incorporating it into the

ABOVE: The 1970s-style wall-to-wall cabinets and dated appliances combined to pretty much overwhelm this modest-size kitchen space.

what was done

- Replaced all cabinets, countertops, and backsplash
- Installed new appliances and integrated them into the cabinetry
- Increased storage by bringing in a standing chest and installing custom wall-hung display cabinets
- Added white bead-board paneling on several walls

OPPOSITE: Hanging open shelves and glass-fronted cabinets display collectibles and add extra storage space. The standing cabinet with an antique pine countertop serves as a buffet sideboard, softening the look of the kitchen.

vintage decor. A microwave, hidden behind a cabinet door, and a dishwasher also became part of the red-cabinet scheme.

By integrating the new kitchen into the old space, Veillette successfully kept the character of the nineteenth-century barn while providing efficient, modern conveniences—a generous mix of old and new.

finishing touches

LEFT: To provide more storage in what is basically a small kitchen, Veillette designed two custom cabinets that fit between the barn's window sashes. Each cabinet includes built-in drawers, plate racks, and shelves to display collectibles.

BELOW, LEFT: The O'Briens opted for a white farmhouse sink, but a more traditional nineteenth-century look could have been achieved with this one, plain except for the handsome filigree design on its molded front.

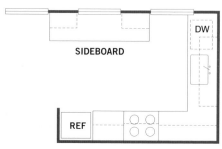

ABOVE: The core of the kitchen's work space measures only 9 by 11 feet, yet the design of the layout makes the room appear much larger.

COLOR TIP

Build a color scheme around permanent items in the room. In this case, the barn's original red door inspired the color choice for the cabinets.

refined rusticity

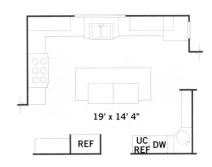

19' x 14' 4"

REF   UC REF   DW

When designer David Heigl was asked to create a kitchen for Pickell Builders Design House, overlooking the shoreline of Lake Geneva, Wisconsin, it was the casual lakefront setting and the summer season that inspired him. "I envisioned kids running through the room with sand on their feet," he recalled. "This is primarily a vacation community, which means that everything is more relaxed here."

Heigl went on to explain that although the kitchen was part of a show house, its design reflected what consumers have been asking for when building or remodeling their own spaces. Topping their list, where kitchens are concerned, is the liberal use of natural materials such as granite or marble, professional-style appliances, and unfitted cabinetry that mimics what Heigl described as "the look of a European country kitchen."

For him, the first order of business was fine-tuning the floor plan to gain storage space. "The biggest challenge

was the open design of the room," he said, explaining that interior walls were eliminated wherever possible to take advantage of the water views. As a result, there were only two walls in the kitchen. "That didn't give us much space for wall cabinets," he pointed out.

He solved the problem by designing a center island within an L-shaped island to establish kitchen boundaries and also provide a self-contained prep area outside the existing work triangle. "The outer island helps to define the space—the cook on one side, family and guests on the other," he said.

Fitted out with a prep sink, a pair of built-in ovens, and a dishwasher, "the center island could become either a mini-kitchen or a wet bar, depending on the user," he declared. "I myself can envision a mom or dad making sandwiches and feeding the kids—still in their bathing suits—right there."

Most kitchen chores would be taken care of at the center island, which features a two-level countertop and spans 9 feet, providing ample room for two or more cooks. With wall space at a premium, the designer was able to tuck two single ovens into one side of the island and outfit the remainder with storage cupboards and drawers. "We

were lucky to have that option," Heigl remarked, in describing the unusual oven configuration. The wall cabinets he succeeded in finding room for are made of a light-toned pine. Before they were installed, each cabinet was carefully hand-rubbed with a dark glaze to simulate the appearance of age.

The focal point of Heigl's kitchen layout is the alcove for the cooktop, with its distinctive zinc hood framed with distressed-fir timbers and hand-carved corbels. To further the old-world flavor, he installed a rugged flagstone floor, like those found in a great many old farmhouses—cool underfoot and amazingly impervious to wear. A vast expanse of white marble covers every available counter surface, an unusual touch in a farmhouse kitchen.

"Most people wouldn't even consider using this much marble, but it's a durable stone and it's also water-resistant," he said. A full complement of stainless steel appliances, including a professional-style cooktop, warming drawer, two dishwashers, and refrigerator round out the amenity package. "It's an interesting mix," said Heigl. "What I really like is the contrast between the rough-hewn elements and the sleek new surfaces and appliances."

BELOW: The silver-toned double sink features an unusual serpentine divider. Glass-fronted doors were added to upper cabinets extended to the ceiling to maximize every inch of storage space.

BELOW: The custom-fabricated zinc exhaust hood was first given an acid wash and then waxed to achieve a weathered patina.

BOTTOM: With two built-in side-by-side single ovens and warming drawers, the center island becomes a cooking powerhouse. The arrangement gives the cook a choice of three handy surfaces on which to rest hot dishes.

BELOW: Leaving small appliances out on the counters would shatter the pleasantly rustic mood of the kitchen. So they are concealed here in a cupboard with a flip-up door.

BOTTOM: Pull-out basket drawers beside the bottom-mount refrigerator add texture and authenticity to the rustic-flavored room.

RIGHT: A well-chosen flourish can complete the look of any farmhouse kitchen. Consider an antique-style faucet to evoke the warmth and romance of the European landscape.

BELOW: Even with a two-level countertop, the island offers ample contiguous work areas. An antique pendant adds needed task lighting.

down-home design

New space, reconfigured
space, more efficient space—from first
concept to final design, a kitchen
remodel is almost always driven by a
need for space. This challenge was met
head on by homeowners Faye and
Richard Rosenberg, in Northbrook,
Illinois, when they began planning an
upgrade to their tiny 1968 kitchen.

With the help of Orren Pickell
Designers and Builders, of Lincoln-
shire, the Rosenbergs added 240 square
feet to the room and 40 percent more
cabinet space in a down-to-earth design
equipped with a host of amenities.

Adding 7 feet along the length of the
kitchen gave the existing space room
to breathe, according to design team
member Jeff Eichhorn. The addition
also supplied just enough room to
accommodate the Rosenbergs' goal of
having a kitchen where everyone could
comfortably gather. "It's amazing how
much you can fit into that amount
of space," Eichhorn exclaimed, "and
with good planning, you can make the
whole space feel bigger."

The shining star of the Rosenberg
kitchen is a grand center island
inspired by Faye's design dare—to
house "everything we could think of
that would fit in." The pine base

incorporates a drawer dishwasher,
old-style glass-fronted storage bins
(for pasta, rice, and dry goods), and a
warming drawer where meals on hold
stay hot. The spacious granite counter
provides ample work space, and a
second kitchen sink convenient to the
refrigerator is ideal for food
preparation.

The practicality of properly used
square footage is enhanced by the
couple's choice of furnishings: low-
maintenance all stainless steel
equipment; easy-care ceramic tile
floors with a forgiving tumbled-stone
finish; and white, Shaker-style
cabinetry to brighten the room mixed
with natural pine to warm it up.

Faye's favorite antique pieces,
discovered while stocking the shelves
of her own antique store, provide a
pop of color against the earth-tone
backdrop. Her ever-changing
collections of bakeware, ceramics, and

RIGHT: Besides storage for kitchen essentials,
the cabinets hold a few surprises: a bread bin
behind a drawer, a dishwasher behind a door,
an appliance garage behind doors under the
microwave. The single-bowl undermount sink
is extra deep, which eases cleanup.

FOLLOWING PAGES: Great style expressed with
simplicity is what gives the kitchen distinction.
It features sophisticated design without
underplaying its appealing farmhouse touches.

BELOW: Faye Rosenberg's enthusiasm for her kitchen begins with the custom glass-fronted hutch, the ideal place to display her collection of antique glassware and ceramics. A focal point in the kitchen, it also services the adjoining dining room.

RIGHT: With an island for prep work, a cleanup area, and a dining table and window seat on the opposite end of the room, this kitchen is set up to be a magnet of activity. It's a great place to hang out, even when snacks or meals aren't being prepared.

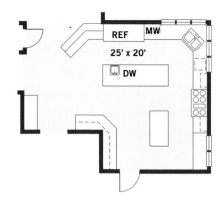

make the farmhouse style yours

RIGHT: For anyone who questioned the primary purpose of the secondary sink, its configuration will erase any doubt. This sink is strictly for meal preparation, with one of its basins designed to hold colanders and bowls. The cutting board comes standard with the sink.

CENTER: Turn on the water and start cooking without making a trip to the sink. A pot-filler faucet, mounted directly above the range, swivels and extends for optimum reach, putting an end to lifting, carrying, and spilling.

BELOW, LEFT: When one dishwasher won't do, add a drawer. Built into the center island and camouflaged with a custom front panel, it offers the option of handling small loads or overflow from the full-size dishwasher next to the main sink.

BELOW, RIGHT: The slide-out bread-box drawer keeps baked goods fresh and is also a handy go-to spot for hungry teenagers or late-night snackers.

glass sparkle behind the glass doors of the built-in hutch. Suspended above the island is Faye's pièce de résistance–a delicate, sparkling chandelier. "It's the first thing I see when I come in the room," she said. "I absolutely love it."

Whether it be the farmhouse ambience, found space for a window seat, the peninsula snack bar, or the sturdy kitchen table, where the family chats about the day's events, they wouldn't change a thing about their kitchen–although they wouldn't mind having more time to spend in it.

recalling the 1950s

BELOW: Set in a niche by the refrigerator, the microwave is convenient but mostly out of sight.

BELOW, CENTER: Flanked by glass-fronted cabinets, the farm sink gleams in daylight from three casement windows and a transom.

BOTTOM: Dappled with browns and golds, the counters echo colors apparent in the flooring, the room's light-colored surfaces, and throughout the predominantly light-colored kitchen.

Arline Gidion had originally dreamed of a kitchen that reflected styles of the eighteenth or early nineteenth century. But when it came time to remodel the kitchen of the East Hampton, New York, house that she and her husband, Peter, used as a weekend retreat, she also realized she liked the kitchens of the 1950s. When it was clear that hers would be a period kitchen, a question arose: which period? None in particular, it turns out, but the result has a charm that is timeless.

Architect Erica Broberg had already remodeled the tiny galley kitchen in the Gidions' New York City apartment and, while creating a vintage look in the weekend kitchen, she was determined to bring in the brightness, airiness, and verdant views that the city kitchen lacked. The

first step was to raise the ceiling to a peak—"A high ceiling is a real treat for city dwellers," Broberg noted—and install large, transom-topped windows overlooking Arline's gardens. The bead-board ceiling and cabinets lend an early American country flavor reinforced by furniture-style legs on base cabinets. Flat doors complete the informal look.

Gidion had her heart set on a cheerful yellow-and-white kitchen, a classic mid-century color scheme. The foundation hue was set by the range, partly enameled and partly stainless steel. Broberg sent a sample chip to the tile maker, who matched its yellow in trim pieces for the backsplash. The room became a perfect backdrop for Gidion's Shawnee, McCoy, and Red Wing pottery—all displayed on shelves Broberg included for that purpose.

OPPOSITE: An open ceiling not only increased the expansive feeling of this kitchen but also bolstered its casual cottage atmosphere. The unusual honey-colored floor is hickory wood; it anchors the room's warm color palette.

RIGHT: Combining elements of U- and L-shaped floor plans, the architect made sure the remodeled space would work well for both kitchen functions and social gatherings.

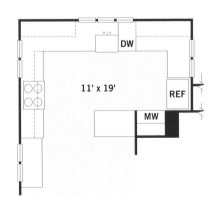

DW

11' x 19'

REF

MW

a passion for color

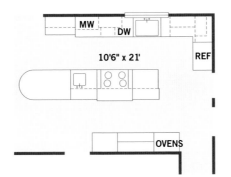

MW | DW | REF
10'6" x 21'
OVENS

LEFT: The new space is considerably smaller than the kitchen the Pannells left behind in Boise. Accordingly, every spare cubic inch of cabinet space is used for storage.

BELOW: Jean Pannell's collection of teacups is lit up behind glass on the non-cooktop side of the island. Behind the solid parts of the doors are serving pieces.

When an unexpected move forced Jean and John Pannell to trade their amenity-laden kitchen in Boise, Idaho, for a lesser-equipped model in Duxbury, Massachusetts, Jean wasted no time jazzing up the outdated space. "I loved the kitchen in our Boise house," she declared. "I was determined to incorporate as many of those features as I could into our new home."

Working with designer Cameron Snyder, of Kitchen Concepts, in Norwell, Massachusetts, the Pannells began by replicating the coffered ceiling they'd had in their previous home. "The coffered ceiling added visual interest and imparted a traditional element to offset the otherwise contemporary feel of the room," Snyder recounted. "It also helped balance the space." In shaping his design, he stayed within the original footprint of the kitchen, but fine-tuned the floor plan, eliminating a peninsula and swapping the locations of the refrigerator and double oven. Snyder then inserted a multilevel island combining both a

cooktop and a prep sink. To create a spot for the Pannells to enjoy informal meals, he equipped the island with a curved table and pull-up seating.

"We rounded off the edges to give it the feeling of a diner," said Jean of the arrangement, which accommodates five people easily. The opposite side of the island acts as a spatial barrier—a row of lighted display cabinets housing Jean's teacup collection, with serving pieces stored below.

Jean proved fearless in her choice of colors and materials, pairing green maple cabinets and sleek black granite countertops against wheat-colored walls. Her fondness for natural materials matched by a high regard

sink cabinets

The apron sink has become a staple of farmhouse and country-kitchen chic. And just as the right frame enhances an artwork, the right cabinets will give a sink the attention it deserves. Sleek, modern cabinets would upstage the humble farmhouse design, but vintage-inspired woodwork and an antique finish can both accommodate a large apron sink and complement its rustic, Provençal charm. Self-contained units like this ageless stand-alone cabinet, with a towel rack, turned legs decorating two corners, and narrow molding strips framing each door's center panel, are produced by a number of manufacturers.

OPPOSITE: The design mixes such traditional elements as fluted moldings and a coffered ceiling with more contemporary-style cabinets.

LEFT: The prep sink location, right next to the cooktop, allows the cook to fill pots with ease and, if desired, rinse oily skillets immediately after cooking.

BELOW: A large-scale farmhouse sink with a bridge faucet is another traditional element in the design. To the left of the basin is a dishwasher with a cabinet panel-covered door that completely hides its controls.

for natural materials: the warm gray, green, and copper colors found in the slate floor. "If I spill something," she confessed, "it's so easy to clean."

Storage proved more difficult, however. With no place to put the walk-in pantry, Snyder committed every available square inch to storage: an appliance garage, pull-out racks and shelving, and roll-out pantry units. "We had to scale down a bit," Jean admitted, "but we managed to fit it all in."

slate show

"With its amazing colors and rugged texture, slate is a good choice when you want a floor that is tough as well as beautiful," said designer Cameron Snyder. "It's as hard as granite, but you don't see the scratches."

Slate is a natural stone whose colorful palette extends to red, green, and copper hues that vary in pattern and intensity. The obvious natural-stone benchmark is granite, which is resistant to most stains and scratches but is also naturally porous and requires a coating of sealant each year to keep it looking good. Upkeep of slate is easy, by contrast—just a simple damp mop does the trick.

great walls of tile

BELOW, LEFT: An irregular checkerboard-patterned installation points up the surreal quality of the Fornasetti-designed faces. Solid black squares allow the eye to rest.

BELOW, RIGHT: A band of gleaming bronze tiles forms the perfect material medium between the black granite counters and light wood cabinets. The horizontal orientation of the tile emphasizes the width of the room.

Since the backsplash is often the first thing someone notices when entering a kitchen, it's a great place to have some fun and let your imagination run wild. A well-designed backsplash can become a design focus and also alleviate some architectural shortcomings in a too-dark, too-small, or too-short kitchen. Here, in various styles, is a quintet of tile backsplash installations, each of which presents unique possibilities.

ABOVE, LEFT: Mixing sizes and shapes within a monochromatic tile collection keeps a backsplash both lively and cohesive.

ABOVE: The large format of these glass tiles minimizes grout lines in the backsplash, an important factor in maintaining a sleek look in a contemporary kitchen. The tile's ribbed lines echo the design of the silver-trimmed storage cabinets above and the slender drawer handles below.

LEFT: Rectangular tiles running upright on a wall can create or enhance the impression of height, even in confined spaces.

beautiful blends

A comfortable mix is the best way to describe kitchens
that embrace both past and present, and include
design elements that could be Swedish or Dutch,
English or French, but actually morph into something
distinctly American. Are there stately columns, an
antique chopping block, a stainless steel range? With
cutting-edge appliances, surfaces, and plumbing,
virtually every new kitchen is a blend. Any mix works
if it doesn't impede a kitchen's functionality. Taste and
scale are the primary determinants.

cinderella story

OPPOSITE: A cluster of columns—both full- and half-height—unify the space and point up the transition from kitchen to dining area in what is essentially one space.

BELOW: A spice garage conveniently placed alongside the cooktop makes it easy to fine-tune seasonings while preparing meals.

Pity this poor stepchild of a kitchen. Because the dining area hogged the room, the kitchen was shunted off to the perimeter. With clever design, however, what was once a relatively remote, isolated area was transformed into a functional boomerang-galley kitchen.

The metamorphosis was no small feat. "The kitchen is actually part of the home's great room, where it is basically confined to one angled wall," said Melissa Smith, CKD, of Hermitage Kitchen Design Gallery, in Franklin, Tennessee. "That's all the space we had to work with, in terms of installing appliances and tall cabinets."

Stuck behind the dining area, some element of the kitchen had to be made to pop out visually or else the room would simply vanish. Smith created a hearth-like cooking alcove to fill that role, and it turned out to be central to her entire kitchen design.

Three factors help the hearth stand out: location, material, and lighting. Smith placed the hearth in the center of the back wall and specified that it be made of stacked stone (actually, a convincing synthetic) to match the fireplace on the other side of the room. The stone stands out effectively from the cabinets, and the lighting further enhances the contrast.

The hearth also taps into Bowling Green homeowner Shirley Scott's love of antiques. Thus, the kitchen includes decorative touches that give it a century-old feel. The cabinets, for example, are painted cherry that is heavily distressed to reveal the wood. "Shirley has a real appreciation of history," Smith commented, "and the finishes reflect that. Take a close look at one of the doors; it looks as if it could have come off an old pie safe."

Moving in that same direction, Smith specified a honed finish on the granite countertops. "It's a nice effect when you're trying to make something that's new look a little bit timeworn," she explained.

Scott not only likes her new kitchen's old-fashioned look, she finds herself endlessly enamored of its newfangled conveniences. The blend of elements works perfectly; not even the modified traditional columns seem out of place.

"My other kitchen may have had more space, but it was not laid out as conveniently," she recalled. "On either side of the cooktop I now have pull-outs to hold all my spices and seasonings, and they're such timesavers—always right there when I'm preparing dishes."

Opposite the powerhouse back wall is a dog-leg prep island with a split-level countertop. This area gets a workout when Scott embarks on a baking binge; the high countertop serves as a buffet when she entertains, which she does frequently.

"It seems like a lot of people have been in and out of the room ever since the kitchen was completed," said Scott. "I find it fun to have company there with me when I'm cooking." And in a welcome twist to the fairy-tale plot, at midnight the new kitchen does not abruptly turn into a pumpkin.

RIGHT: The contemporary open floor plan of this kitchen is surprisingly compatible with the room's traditional style.

BELOW: From its arched faux-stone "firebox" opening to the carved-wood mantel detail, a traditional hearth is reinterpreted as the surround for a five-burner gas cooktop.

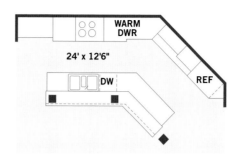

RIGHT: A pull-out faucet eliminates the need for a separate veggie sprayer—a constructive step away from the overcrowded sink deck.

BELOW: Tall appliance installations, like the refrigerator and exhaust hood, had to be located on the "inside" wall of the kitchen to avoid blocking the view to the adjoining dining area.

simply beachy

Cooking and eating with a view of the Chesapeake Bay can be a wondrous experience, which is why these homeowners positioned their kitchen where they did. In a house on a rolling acre overlooking the bay, they put the heart of the home where they could watch the water. Kitchen designer Mark T. White, of Kitchen Encounters, in Annapolis, Maryland, picked up on the essence of this predetermined space by accenting the colors of sand. His real accomplishment, though, was ferreting out exactly what the family needed in order to make this kitchen a place where they could cook, eat, entertain, and just have a great time.

Signing on after the four-bedroom house had already been designed, White played catch-up through in-depth interviews. (Architect Scarlett Breeding, of Alt/Breeding Architects, in Annapolis, had already cultivated a relationship with Pat, one of the homeowners.) "Mark did a detailed survey," Pat recalled. "He asked questions to find out how we liked

to live in our kitchen, how we cook, and even whether the principal cook—that would be me—was right- or left-handed." Digesting his survey results, White conceived four different plans. His clients had no trouble deciding which one suited them best.

"This is a house without halls," Pat declared, pointing out that the kitchen is visible from both the adjacent dining room and the windowed breakfast room. "We had to make sure what we did in the kitchen complemented both of those areas," said White.

The plan he conceived was based on an L-shaped arrangement of appliances and counters, to which he added a huge island with a curved breakfast bar on one side and a work surface arranged in a lazy Z pattern on the other.

"My clients didn't want anything fussy or ornate," White explained. So he helped them choose semicustom cabinets with recessed-panel doors in the Shaker style along with pewter-finish pulls. "We used maple with a light-colored stain that was softened further by a white glaze," he explained. "As the house was to be built beside the bay, the owners wanted to establish a beach-like feeling. For the doors on the lower cabinets, for example, we used

OPPOSITE: Pale wood cabinets with beaded panels team up with additional breezy colors to create a beach-home feel in the main kitchen area. That seaside essence becomes inescapable in the octagonal breakfast room, where water views are apparent through every window.

BELOW: Thirsty swimmers need not splash into the kitchen for refreshments, thanks to the undercounter beverage cooler at the end of the island. Note the curve in the dining counter, which offers relief from straight lines in the rest of the space. This kitchen also addresses whether an oven and a refrigerator can be installed beside each other. The answer: yes.

BELOW, RIGHT: The island seating area is directly opposite the cooktop to encourage interaction with the cook. In the background, stacked cabinets and heavy white molding carry the eye all the way to the high ceiling. At the far right (toward the bottom of the picture), a glass-door cabinet wedged between two columns formally separates the kitchen from the dining room.

eating options

Despite the seductive nature of the octagonal breakfast room, designer Mark T. White knew his clients wanted a space within their compact kitchen for quick meals and snacks. That is why he created a raised bar on one side of the island and made it big enough to accommodate two stools.

"Our guests tend to hang out there," said Pat, "and my husband likes to be in the kitchen to socialize while I'm cooking." The designer created an island well equipped for multitasking. There is a vegetable sink, a beverage center, and a cooktop with downdraft ventilation—all either cut into or placed below the granite countertops. Stool diners and kibitzers look into the kitchen; the cook enjoys the water view.

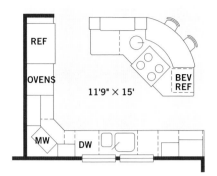

REF

OVENS

11'9" × 15'

BEV REF

MW   DW

LEFT: Although the space leads out to a deck and pool, smartly arranged work and storage areas keep traffic manageable. The island acts as centerpiece and primary traffic governor.

BELOW: This sink, stationed beside the cooktop, is an ideal spot to fill pots with water for pasta or stock, or to serve as a traditional prep sink for washing a variety of vegetables.

BELOW: To break up the mass of wood cabinets, some of the doors have faux-mullion glass panel insets. Air bubbles in the glass add texture and amp up visual interest.

BOTTOM: The dishwasher is fully integrated—meaning that it is invisible when closed—thanks to the cabinet panel and the fact that the controls are situated on top of the door.

bead board as the center panels; it complements the bead board we applied to both sides of the island's raised section, where the stools pull up.

"Because there would be so many upper cabinets, and we didn't want a look that was too busy, we avoided putting bead board there," he added. "Instead, we used plain, flat-center panels plus a few glass-fronted doors to break up the mass."

White optimized the space by installing cabinetry all the way up to the wide crown molding just below the ceiling. The molding matched woodwork that appears in most of the other rooms. The owners conceded that the top row of their new kitchen cabinets is hard to reach. "We store things there that we don't use often," said Pat, invoking a smart-storage dictum. The red-oak floor that borders the kitchen also flows into the breakfast room. Within the kitchen proper, limestone floor tile extends the pale palette set by the cabinets. Punctuating the space, like floor-to-ceiling sculptures, are a pair of columns that the owners explain are only decorative. The designer used them to bracket a raised cabinet with glass doors that faces the dining room.

"It's convenient to keep glassware and crystal there. The back side of the cabinet steps down to the island countertop, giving me more work space." The kitchen also functions as the entertaining hub of the house. In addition to windows overlooking the bay, French doors lead out to a deck and pool. The room gets more than its share of traffic, but its efficient arrangement of work and storage areas never feels compromised.

"By the time our house plan was finalized, we realized that we had lost some closet space because of the open floor plan," Pat recalled. "We were aware we needed to squeeze as much storage as we could into the kitchen. Overall, the space looks and feels bigger than it is. For us, it's awesome."

day in, day out

OPPOSITE: Locating the range in the island keeps cooking activities central to the room and also preserves access to the view. Even the storage armoire is completely sided with glass.

BELOW: There's no shortage of dining options in this kitchen design. In addition to casual seating at the island, there is a formal eating area as well as an L-shaped banquette—complete with fireplace—on two sides of the room.

When designer Elizabeth

Spengler was working on this eclectic farmhouse kitchen, overlooking a private airstrip near Tucson, Arizona, she knew exactly what the client wanted in the room—because she herself was the client.

"It had to be cozy and comfortable," said Elizabeth, of the inviting Aussie-inspired farmhouse she shares with her husband Bob. Elizabeth's challenge was twofold. She not only had to execute a successful design but one that could hold its own against a backdrop of soaring planes and spectacular views of the Catalina mountains.

The finished space is as exceptional as the view and every bit as exuberant as its owners. The room's generous 23-by-28-foot dimensions make it perfect for entertaining, offering a choice of dining areas, indulgently long stretches of countertop, and a full array of professional-style appliances. The island is topped with a curved stone slab and equipped with two dishwashers and a 60-inch range.

Hovering above the range is a Danish-made ventilation hood that Elizabeth chose for its sculptural shape and custom details, including a built-in pot rack and end shelving.

"I like having things handy when I cook," she explained.

While the island is the workhorse of the room, it also serves as the anchor point for a major storage component in the kitchen. Because installing a run of view-framing windows meant sacrificing a complete wall of upper cabinets, other provisions for storage had to be made. Elizabeth solved the problem by designing a folksy, hand-painted bonnet-topped armoire that accommodates dishes, glasses, and silverware. "It opens on all four sides and can be loaded easily from the dishwasher," she added.

A fan and collector of MacKenzie-Childs pottery, she commissioned a decorative painter to incorporate several of its motifs—the colorful guinea fowl, familiar checkerboards, and a diamond pattern—against a potent palette of apple-green and red for the freestanding cabinet. At her request, the artist included the couple's initials and wedding year. "Personalizing the piece in this way makes it even more special," she said.

Notable is the mix of finishes that contribute to the sprightly atmosphere. The arcing island top is fabricated from a slab of French lava stone that has

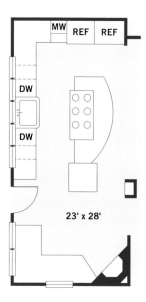

23' x 28'

been glazed, fired, and given a crackled finish. "What's nice about this surfacing," the designer added, "is that there are no grout joints. It doesn't have to be sealed like some other materials. Scorching is never a problem, either." A 10-by-12-foot breakfast nook features a corner banquette with upholstered seating, inviting family and friends to take advantage of the view. Equipped with a cozy gas fireplace and within reach of both the espresso machine and an all-in-one breakfast station, it is now the couple's favorite place to sip coffee or relax with a glass of wine. According to Elizabeth, "We start and end the day right here."

BELOW: When not needed, cooking ingredients and small appliances are organized and stored out of sight in the compact baking station located between the sink and the microwave.

BOTTOM, LEFT: A double-bowl apron-front sink coupled with a bridge-style faucet suit the kitchen's stylishly rustic ambience. So do the double-hung windows and bead-board walls.

BOTTOM, RIGHT: An awkward space in a corner becomes an essential asset when fitted with a deep utility sink, an auxiliary work surface, and an arrangement of cabinets and drawers.

design points

ABOVE: When you know your storage needs thoroughly, it's not difficult to customize your cabinets accordingly. Produce compartments in cool, ventilated drawers let you keep staples fresh and specifically where they are needed.

BELOW: Pull-and-pivot shelves make the contents of corner cabinets easily accessible to the cook—no more scrounging in those deep, dark recesses.

BELOW, LEFT: An exuberant design element, the armoire opens on all four sides. Note how the band of red diamonds at its midsection echoes the control knobs on the front of the range.

BELOW, RIGHT: Cheery colors and collectibles brighten the banquette area. This dining nook, situated beside an oval-topped raised fireplace, enjoys both a view of the outdoors and a close connection to the kitchen.

color power

"Having gone to school and lived in Mexico, my client wanted to use authentic Mexican color combinations," said Douglas W. Burdge, AIA, of Burdge & Associates Architects, in Malibu, California. After laying out a 10-by-20-foot eat-in kitchen, the architect escorted his clients to Mexico to hand-pick the Talavera tile that eventually covered the walls, the base of the island, and the main countertop.

"It's a blue-and-white glazed ceramic tile in a traditional Mexican pattern," according to Burdge, who created a space where the homeowners could cook, dine, work, and entertain. The kitchen, which flows into the food pantry and butler's pantry as well as the family room, overlooks a covered patio whose roof extends from the antique barn beams that span the

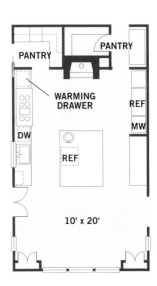

LEFT: The space is filled with features typically found in Mexican kitchens: colorful tile-covered walls, counter units, and countertops; a floor made of Cantera, a quarried Mexican stone; and a fireplace set in a plain plaster surround.

ABOVE, RIGHT: The kitchen is sizable, with work areas arranged around the island hub.

RIGHT: Pocket doors hide the TV when it is not in use; an awning door can be lowered to conceal the microwave in a floor-to-ceiling storage unit beside the built-in desk. From the desk it is possible to look over a tile-faced partition into the adjacent family room.

BELOW: A glass-topped table, surrounded by wood-and-leather chairs, dominates one end of the kitchen, where lush gardens can be seen through a wall of windows. Beside the banquette is a built-in bench for extra seating and storage.

OPPOSITE: Salvaged antique barn beams not only adorn the ceiling but also frame the built-in exhaust hood over the range. Beyond the range and warming drawer is the butler's pantry, complete with a wine cooler and refrigerator.

width of the kitchen. The kitchen's cabinets are knotty alder, distressed to show age. Other elements mix new and old—local finds, and some imported pieces. The owners' Mexican art enriches the space.

tile lore

- The most significant difference between tile made in Europe and the U.S. and tile from Mexico is that the former is generally porcelain based; 90 percent of the latter is clay.

- Clay-based tile is more porous and may not be as durable as porcelain. In addition, porcelain tiles are machine made; clay-based tiles are often handmade.

- To create a practical countertop surface, use ⅜-inch-thick clay tiles, hardy enough to avert cracking if something heavy is dropped on them. Tile on walls and cabinet facings can be ¼ inch thick.

- Since it is often handmade, clay-based tile may not be uniform. Size irregularities can be compensated for by the way grout is applied.

- Glass tiles, though not used here, have grown in popularity. Tougher than clay-based tile, glass may not be quite as durable as porcelain-based ceramics.

long-term investment

ABOVE: Parties put a big strain on the small size of the old galley kitchen. The update is basically a wider version of a galley—with more efficient amenities and a convenient spot for the dining table, plus a lot more flexibility.

OPPOSITE: A heavily insulated French range forges an impressive presence and is also the culinary powerhouse of the kitchen. "It's built solid, like a vault," said homeowner Johnson.

BELOW: Accessories render almost every cubic inch of this pantry functional. The wire rack in the main compartment creates a veritable merry-go-round of cooking staples; slide-out bins provide access to items stashed way back in the cabinet.

When Gregory Johnson described his kitchen as "built for sound," he was not referring to its acoustics. While jam sessions happen regularly in his Victorian home in San Francisco's Haight-Ashbury district, they are strictly of the culinary variety. "We like to invite people over to cook as a social activity, and we needed a place that could comfortably accommodate our friends," said Johnson, recalling a recent gathering celebrating a bumper crop of Meyer lemons. "Everyone pitched in and we had a great time." That kitchen work party yielded a tasty lemon curd along with several batches of sorbet and pungent limoncello aperitif. "We do things like that all the time," he declared. As entertaining needs escalated, their outdated galley kitchen strained to keep up. Fortunately, Johnson and his wife, Michelle Morainvillers, knew what had to be done. Now retired, both had worked in professional kitchens—he cooked up patés and confits for a well-known Parisian caterer, while she flourished as a pastry chef—so they undertook the remodeling project, with Johnson acting as general contractor.

Although the footprint of the 130-square-foot kitchen remained the same, structural changes expanded the cramped dining room and provided enough space for an 80-square-foot outdoor terrace. Dominating the cooking area is a hefty European commercial range with a variety of burners (including a French top) and dual ovens. To the right of the range, a built-in stainless steel tower corrals a collection of mixing bowls. Open shelves replace wall-hung cabinets, providing ready access to their contents. "Isn't it easier to just grab plates and glasses and put them on the table?" Johnson asked. A collection of well-used copper cookware, purchased during the couple's frequent trips to France, hangs within easy reach of the range. "We lugged them home in our suitcases a piece at a time."

Johnson insisted on durable, easy-to-maintain surfaces similar to those found in the Italian cafés he had visited. The materials he chose—butcher block, marble, and stainless steel—contribute to the kitchen's professional ambience, but their aesthetic benefits do not stop at installation. "The limestone and marble pick up a wonderful patina over time," he added.

The floor planks are salvaged

BELOW: Made of stainless steel, the double-basin sink is deep enough to hold the owners' largest pot—a giant used for canning. To the left of the sink, knives slip neatly into designated slots in the 48-inch butcher-block slab.

design points

A kitchen that sees plenty of cooking and entertaining needs some robust equipment and spaces to keep everything. Here's what the design team did for this kitchen:

Prep LEFT: To wash fresh produce, the double-bowl stainless steel sink includes a perforated insert, also stainless, that serves as a colander. The insert covers virtually the entire bowl area and can be removed effortlessly for cleaning.

Cook ABOVE, LEFT: Making a batch of preserves can use up a lot of bowls. These stainless steel shelves nestled next to the range provide storage that's abundant, easily cleaned, and conveniently placed.

Store ABOVE, RIGHT: Generous divided drawers keep spices and condiments in one handy place. The size helps, too. It saves time if you only have to open one drawer instead of two.

California bay laurel; the cabinets crafted of redwood slabs culled from 800-year-old trees in nearby Mendocino, accented with claro walnut trim. Upon viewing the virgin wood recovered from the forest floor, the owners resisted the urge to chop it up for cabinetry. Instead, they devised a slim pull-out pantry that strategically incorporated the 8-foot

BELOW, LEFT: Open shelves rule this kitchen's walls. In addition to lightening the look by eliminating wall cabinets, they make dishes easier to take down and put away.

BELOW: Massive expanses of glass make the eating area a treasure. The high shelves around the perimeter are a perfect perch for display items and audio equipment (in the corner).

boards as door panels. Salvaged wood presents special challenges, however, as the couple's cabinetmaker, Ken Seidman, of Seidman Woodworks, in San Francisco, discovered. "As it doesn't come in standard sizes," Seidman reported, "it's more difficult to cut, mill, and plane." In addition, redwood is a soft wood that dents easily, making it an unorthodox cabinet choice. To stabilize the large doors, Seidman glued the ¼-inch panels to plywood backing for extra support. "It's harder to utilize, but the end result is beautiful," he said, noting that the owners fully embraced the wood's imperfections. Moreover, the couple couldn't be happier with the results. "This is timeless design that will last for another twenty-five years," Johnson said. "We are never going to rip this kitchen out."

elegant improvement

OPPOSITE: Off-white painted and glazed cabinets lay the foundation for the Victorian look that befits this kitchen in a landmark building. Even the brand-new pendant task lights were selected to contribute to the room's vintage flavor.

BELOW, TOP: On either side of the range, the cabinets descend all the way to the countertop, yet Sherry still craved counter space to work on. Since these cabinets are only 9 inches deep, they are used to store herbs and spices.

BELOW, CENTER: Adjacent to the spice cabinet in one corner is a small-appliance cabinet. This is not an ordinary appliance repository, however; it was designed to fill precious corner space that might otherwise have been wasted.

BELOW, BOTTOM: The drawer refrigerator keeps drinks and other cold staples handy. Note that the granite countertop steps down here—from 37¼ inches (a comfortable level for tall users) to the standard 36-inch height.

Sherry Samsing's kitchen

in suburban Annapolis, Maryland, was everything she needed it to be: light and airy, with new appliances and plenty of storage for an ever-expanding glassware and china collection. What's more, Samsing recalled, "there was really room to roam." Despite the room's near perfection, Samsing would soon be roaming permanently—away from that spacious kitchen. Her husband, John Pilli, a local builder, discovered a bargain he could not resist: a Victorian brownstone in need of special extra care on a prime downtown street. "At first I was hesitant about moving," said Samsing, "but the more I thought about it, the more smitten I was. There was something about the house that captured me emotionally."

So the couple bought the landmark-status building and set about turning it into a home. The process required a call to friend and kitchen designer Mark T. White, KD, of Kitchen Encounters, in Annapolis. "Sherry loved the home but had some concerns about scaling back to a much smaller kitchen," White remembered. "It was my job to help her figure out how to do this."

To that end, White gently altered the

save room for more

Customizing kitchen cabinets can transform a small space into one that is big on storage, said designer Mark T. White. Here are some ideas:

Come down a notch Bring wall cabinets down to counter level, and use them to hide small appliances and other counter clutter.

Make every inch count Build spice storage around the range or cooktop. Have a designer create a custom exhaust-hood alcove with a storage shelf for pots and pans.

Kick it up Run cabinets all the way to the ceiling. Use the upper, tough-to-reach shelves for seasonal items, such as Grandma's Christmas dishes.

Think access Fit key base cabinets with glide-out shelves or trays that allow you to quickly reach items stored way in the back.

existing area by combining it with a small adjoining dining room to create a 257-square-foot space. "The couple wanted to modernize their new home," he said, "but at the same time were eager to maintain the classic Victorian character that made it appealing."

He also tweaked the flow of foot traffic into and out of the space by closing off the doorway that connected the kitchen to the front hall. In its place, he installed a full-size built-in refrigerator with display storage overhead. This move not only improved the traffic pattern but also provided extra storage for Samsing's dish

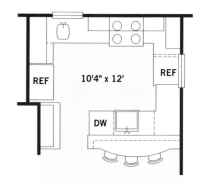

LEFT AND BELOW: Nineteenth-century charm meets modern practicality. Samsing and Pilli picked products that were quaint and Victorian for the most part, including the farmhouse sink with vintage-style faucet, pull-out spray, and handy detergent dispenser. To the right of the sink is a dishwasher behind a cabinet panel. A subtle change: This entire stretch of countertop sits an inch and a half higher than usual to accommodate its tall users.

RIGHT: This deceptively simple plan actually has two readily discernible work triangles and could easily accommodate three users at once.

REF   10'4" x 12'   REF

DW

collection. Another trick White used to help his clients make the most of their compact kitchen was to design towering, 10-foot-tall furniture-style cabinets. Because the cabinets were custom, White could rest the wall cabinets on the counter instead of stopping them 18 inches above. "I asked that the cabinets go all the way to the ceiling so I would have plenty of storage for dishes. I needed a place to put such things as holiday china, which

I like to use, but not every day. The very top cabinets are perfect for this," Samsing recalls. She takes her dish fascination both seriously and with a dash of humor. "I have several sets of everyday dishes and also china patterns that I use only on holidays," she reported. "I always tell myself that I'm not going to buy more, but then I see a pattern I like, and I end up bringing it home. I guess I have a dish fetish." Since the couple likes to

entertain, White provided plenty of places for people to gather, including a cozy seating area opposite the breakfast bar. "The room is small, but not claustrophobic," the designer said. "The U-shaped design solved the space crunch by creating distinct areas for the cook and for guests." White's efforts also helped his clients relinquish any remorse for having left behind a perfectly serviceable kitchen in the 'burbs.

BELOW: Above the range are two display shelves that conceal the ventilation unit and ductwork. The leaded-glass cabinet doors at the far right are another feature of Victorian decor.

RIGHT: As one of the conditions of purchasing the landmark building, the local historical society would not permit the owners to alter any windows. That explains why the one behind the sink drops a few inches to the windowsill below.

FAR RIGHT: Samsing found and immediately purchased an intact mural of glazed ceramic tile to use as the backsplash behind the range.

taste heightened

OPPOSITE: By placing a pair of pantry doors over the structural column in the kitchen, Donohue elongated the space, while creating a usable shallow cabinet for spices. "I don't need a lot of bells and whistles," said homeowner Marianita Meyer. "But I wanted a good stove because we cook a lot."

BELOW: As seen from the dining room, the kitchen was sorely in need of an update.

Like the subject of an episode of a what-not-to-wear TV show, the tiny New York City co-op needed a style makeover. First, the entry was cramped and confining—just inside the front door was a wall blocking sight lines. To the left, another wall, angled across the floor, housed a poorly placed closet. The dining room's mirrored walls created the dizzying effect of a carnival ride. And the ceiling fixture suffered from what could be described as enthusiastic bad taste.

But the building itself had good bones. Starting life as office space in 1929, it had been converted to residential housing during an era of superficial veneers. "Everything was artificial back then," said Marianita Meyer. So when she and her husband, Robert Spragg, bought the apartment, she started updating with paint.

It soon became apparent, however, that expanding the color palette would not be enough to open up the spaces. Bigger changes were needed. Painters at work in the apartment recommended Clare Donohue, a kitchen and bath designer with a flair for carving more out of less. All it took was for Meyer's husband to say, "You're in charge," and she made her move.

Sharing her ideas with Donohue proved easy. "We have the same sensibilities," Meyer pointed out. But the little buttoned-down, black-and-white kitchen she initially envisioned changed when she came across an eggplant-colored commercial-style range. That was the jumping-off point Donohue needed to establish the kitchen's jazzy plum-and-green color scheme. To that she added a custom copper sink, oil-rubbed bronze faucet and cabinet pulls, and a pale-green-glass tile backsplash accented with a border of eggplant and pale-lilac tiles. "All of the materials blend well," said Donohue.

Choosing a look was one issue; redirecting the traffic flow was another. Instead of a path through the dining room to the kitchen, Donohue closed off that route with a half-wall, then carved a doorway from the front hallway, creating a view into the kitchen. Raising the ceilings to 11 feet resulted in a more open ambience; it also created more vertical storage space.

Another challenge Donohue faced was settling on a design that integrated the couple's Mission-style furniture with the remodel. The large, chunky

what was done

- Gutted the kitchen and reoriented its entrance
- Tore out dropped ceilings in the kitchen and dining room and raised them to 11 feet
- Removed glued-down wood parquet floor tiles and replaced them with multicolored slate
- Eliminated a clumsily angled closet in the entry
- Added just over 12 square feet to the kitchen, but more than doubled the storage space
- Added all new cabinetry and green granite counters

pieces were darker than where the kitchen was heading. "But you have to make things work," Donohue declared. "So we took the Mission style and balanced it with modern, using simple white cabinets." The same style repeats in the living room in a wall of custom built-in storage and display units.

In the kitchen, the couple combined storage with display for more efficiency and sophistication. Donohue designed the 10-by-15-foot walnut wall setup to maximize the home's square footage. "The mass was reduced by integrating it into the wall," she explained. "And giving the walnut a two-tone stain kept it fresher, more contemporary." The final upgrade involved unifying floors throughout with varying hues of slate set in a staggered pattern.

Even after spending five months in remodeling limbo, Meyer seemed undaunted: "I still look at the kitchen and smile. It makes me so happy."

BELOW, LEFT: Like a jewel box, the new kitchen is striking for its size, but it's functional, too, thanks to increased storage and up-to-date appliances.

BELOW, RIGHT: A half-wall between the kitchen and dining room creates a giant pass-through, replacing what had been a wide-open walkway with a more intimate connection.

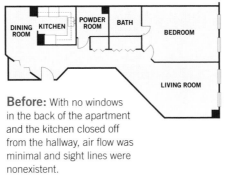

Before: With no windows in the back of the apartment and the kitchen closed off from the hallway, air flow was minimal and sight lines were nonexistent.

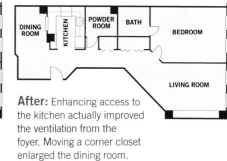

After: Enhancing access to the kitchen actually improved the ventilation from the foyer. Moving a corner closet enlarged the dining room.

seeing the light

Sunlight is no longer the luxury it once was in home design, when its presence was confined mostly to stingily placed, relatively small windows.

Today, because of insulated windows that hold the heat, shut out the cold, and vice versa, it is possible to add them generously almost anywhere. The kitchen presents particular challenges and demands, however.

window options

Architects, kitchen designers, and contractors tend to agree that casement windows are the best choice over a kitchen sink. As they are controlled by a crank, there is no need for anyone to stretch a torso over a 24-inch depth to raise and lower a window. Note, however, that...

- because they open out, casements are more vulnerable to weather damage;

- if a casement's latch release is placed very high, opening and closing that window will be no easier than operating a double-hung;

- you can leave double-hung windows open a bit during a storm without fear of exposing the windows themselves to the elements;

- a tilt window could be a reasonable alternative to a casement. Its lower sash opens in as much as out and is a little easier to deal with than that of a double-hung.

sunlight stretchers

There are a number of ways to bring additional natural light into a kitchen without adding windows that would reduce cabinet or storage space:

- half-rounds can be installed above casement or double-hung windows if there is room;

- boxed-out windows function like bays to create a feeling of expanded indoor space;

- eyebrow windows and transoms are other ways to capture sunlight.

To add light to a kitchen without altering total window design, many architects opt for accessible roof windows or for skylights. To use either, of course, you must have a one-story house or a kitchen extension. A skylight isn't as obtrusive as additional windows. If yours is a dark kitchen that you don't wish to alter significantly, a skylight could be the answer, as it will pull in more sunlight without compromising the architecture of your home.

Most skylights and roof windows come with tinted glass that greatly reduces the heat impact in a room, and there are a spate of interior devices–blinds or louvers–that provide additional shading. Controls of the windows themselves and the shading devices can be manual or electric.

An alternative to these ceiling cutouts are clerestory windows: high-placed horizontal windows that don't compromise or reduce wall space. Because of their placement, they function like skylights in letting the sun penetrate a room, but they don't allow the summer sun to beat down. Clerestories that face south are easily protected in the summer because the sun is high. In the winter, when you want more light, it flows deep into a room.

doors as windows

Because the kitchen is so often linked to a family room, informal dining area, or great room, there must be access through it to the outside or to other parts of the house. That's why French doors have enjoyed a successful revival. Note that such doors need swing space, but if you don't have it, sliders can be a workable alternative. The overriding virtues of sliders are that they just disappear when opened, and their screens operate more easily than those on French doors.

In many homes the kitchen has replaced the living room as the central gathering place, but though it may flow into a family dining space or a great room, the kitchen is still primarily a work space. In considering window and door options that will add natural light and also bring the outdoors in, keep in mind that windows in particular must compete with cabinets and useful storage for wall space. When planning to install French doors or sliders, think carefully about new traffic patterns; make sure they don't interrupt or flow through work areas.

In any kitchen redo, storage needs and unimpeded work space should be prime priorities. The more windows you have, the less space there will be for upper cabinets. And adding doors not only eliminates storage and work space but also encourages traffic. Not even the calmest cook wants to make dinner in the middle of a two-lane highway.

improving the flow

Have you ever cooked a holiday meal while hordes of children—yours and your guests'—trooped through your kitchen? Are you ever foot-tired, hauling food from refrigerator to sink, counter to wall oven, wall oven to cutting board? A big kitchen may have space for every appliance and amenity but still be inefficient because of a poor layout. So, if you plan to redo your kitchen, consider upgrading traffic flow.

Family cooking habits—that is, who cooks—will be important in determining the right design. If there is one primary cook, the arrangement will differ from the kitchen in which both spouses are serious chefs. In the former case, a simple work triangle—range, refrigerator, and sink—might be sufficient; in the latter, two distinct work triangles could be needed. A good, workable layout depends not only on who works in the kitchen but also on what they do there: Are they engaged in meal preparation or just heating foods bought on the way home from work?

stretching the triangle

Kitchen design has been transformed. New technology has subdivided ranges into wall ovens and cooktops; full-size freezers are often separated from refrigerators; microwaves, trash compactors, and in a great many homes one or more dishwashers have become essentials. In addition to having separate pastry counters and recipe-planning desks equipped with computers, a vast number of new and remodeled kitchens are also equipped for recycling.

With all this expansion, in many cases the basic work triangle has been stretched, bent, or just ignored. The best solution, however, involves dual or triple triangles that may overlap or be entirely separate. One triangle might lead from refrigerator to veggie sink to cooktop, for example; another might flow from a wall oven to the main sink to the refrigerator.

As kitchen geometry becomes more complex and kitchen size and traffic flow expand, organization becomes more challenging. Most designers agree that a big kitchen must be even better organized than a small one. Many consumers regard big kitchens as a series of zones: work zone, eating zone, relaxing zone—the latter with comfortable seating.

Add to this trio another design element that has grown rapidly in popularity: the work island. It increases kitchen efficiency, provides another work surface, and shortens the number of steps between zones. A work island also offers the opportunity to include a second sink in a kitchen's design and, where appropriate, a second dishwasher as well. In some kitchens, the island has a built-in cooktop instead of or along with an auxiliary sink. And if there is room, the island can be shared space—a work zone on one side, a dining zone on the other. Most important, an island anchors the space.

directing traffic

Most kitchens have one of the following layouts: one wall, a galley arrangement (a corridor with cabinets and appliances on facing walls) or a U- or L-shaped arrangement, the latter being the most flexible.

The most problematic configuration may be the galley kitchen, because the primary work zone is in the middle of the traffic flow. A U shape contains a work triangle inside the U, a good way to keep non-cooks and hangers-on out of the action. Some cooks favor including a peninsula instead of an island. Either will provide a welcome barrier between the work zone and other areas. With the cook on one side and the hangers-on on the other, the cook can do the main job while guests chop vegetables, toss the salad, or chat.

Any kitchen layout, regardless of its basic shape, can be plagued by traffic-flow problems if the room has too many doorways or the doorways are poorly placed. If a door, or doors, interferes with a work triangle, the solution may be to move the doorway. This can redirect traffic as well as create counter space or position it better relative to the work triangle.

The most important consideration in determining how a kitchen should be designed is how a family plans to live in the space. Patterns of living inevitably pull design in its wake. Design always follows; it never leads.

organizing tips

Clutter plays no favorites. It can occur in pantries or pantry cabinets; it can accumulate in laundry rooms; and, of course, its major haunt is the kitchen. Today's kitchens—where families gather for most meals and guests hover during parties—are as much of a showcase as living rooms and parlors once were. They should be neat, uncluttered, and organized. But before you begin to clear out or clean up yours, stand back and take a long, hard look not only at your kitchen but also at your pantry and laundry room.

Would a helpful guest know where, logically, to locate a spatula, frying pan, blender, or serving tray? Is there enough counter space for prep work? Is there wasted space above wall cabinets or in the corners of base cabinets that could be commandeered to add more storage? Perhaps the best way to de-clutter these cluttered hot spots is to involve the whole family in reestablishing order.

getting started

- Before making any plans or decisions, empty the kitchen, pantry, and laundry room completely—as though you were about to move. Work from the kitchen and pantry to the laundry room. And do the job in stages, focusing first on wall cabinets, then base cabinets, drawers, and finally the refrigerator.

- Sort the contents, separating canned and packaged foods, cleaning gear and laundry products, cookware, and tableware.

- Examine every item; get rid of anything you don't use regularly or haven't touched in years.

- Check for needless duplications (how many sponges or bottles of bleach do you need, for example?). Usable but unwanted items should be shared with neighbors or given to a local senior center or homeless shelter.

- Be prepared to toss anything opened, damaged, or past its printed "use-by" date. Get rid of herbs and spices that have been around a long time.

- Empty the refrigerator storage cabinets. Clean each space thoroughly before putting anything back.

- Consider painting cabinet and drawer interiors in a high-gloss finish or giving them a coat of polyurethane (if made of wood) so they can be wiped clean easily.

- Put back only those items you know you will use; organize according to where you are likely to use them—spices, utensils, and cookware near your range or cooktop, for example.

maximize available space

You may not be in a position to double the size of your kitchen, but you can certainly increase its storage volume. Before refilling shelves and drawers, consider how you can expand their capacity, and try to liberate work surfaces.

- Use cup hooks or under-shelf cup hangers to free up space on shelves.

- Hang knives on a magnetic bar or in an undercabinet storage block.

- Use dividers to increase drawer capacity and keep contents tidy.

- Turn an underutilized closet into a pantry and maximize storage with pullout racks.

- Choose food-storage containers that are square rather than round; they fit better in corners and stack more readily.

- Install slide-out base-cabinet shelving to make cookware more accessible and easier to store. Consider adding carousels to make the most of corner cabinets.

- Hang peg-board panels or stainless steel wall systems to keep most-used cookware and utensils close to where they are needed.

- Open up a closed soffit area and add storage units with glass doors.

- Add a rack to the side of an island to hold tools and utensils, or hooks for kitchen towels.

- Install a flip-out drawer in the front of a sink or a shallow storage drawer in the toe-kick of a base cabinet.

- To help de-clutter the laundry room, install a shelf right above or beside your washer and dryer. This way, your detergent, bleach, stain remover, and dryer sheets will always be easily reached.

reorganize logically

The best way to liberate space is to get stored items off of flat surfaces. If you keep things on a table, a countertop, or a washing machine, you inevitably create clutter. But if you store things vertically—on shelves or in cubes stacked on shelves—the look will be more organized.

In general, things tend to get dis-organized not only where there is too much stuff, but also when stuff doesn't get put away where it belongs—or at all. When reorganizing any space, keep in mind where you most often use items, and store them there. The key to maintaining order is to have everything where you need it. That is the best way to conserve space, save time, and shorten your steps.

laundry room musts

- A laundry basket, hamper, or rolling cart that can alternately hold soiled and clean items. A two- or three-unit container would be ideal so that clothes can be separated.

- A flat surface, counter, or smooth-top appliance on which clean laundry can be sorted and folded.

- Shelving, cabinets, or baskets to hold laundry staples.

- A wall rack to house an iron and ironing board, or an ironing center with a fold-down ironing board.

what's custom? what's not?

True custom cabinets are designed and built from scratch; they can be costly and take weeks or months to produce. You may have clipped a picture in a design magazine that you take to a local millwork or cabinetry shop and say, "This is the kind of kitchen cabinets I want" and hope you can afford the price tag.

Unless you know the cabinetmaker, however—by reputation, by personal recommendation, or from a previous experience—you cannot always be sure of getting solid construction and quality workmanship. In other words, with custom you're pretty much on your own.

With cabinet-shop cabinets, truly one-of-a-kind design is possible, using any wood, laminate finish, or door style, and unusual sizes and touches can be accommodated. It is even possible to specify carefully matched grains and wood from the same tree. But keep in mind that quality varies, depending upon the skills of the individual craftsman or his shop, but the cost is certain to be higher than so-called factory custom.

Most of today's so-called custom cabinetry fits the category of factory custom, in which selections are usually made from existing designs and products. What is finally delivered is rarely the work of a single shop or craftsman but is usually backed by warranty.

Broad but not unlimited choice, then, is what distinguishes most cabinets sold today as custom. They may not be wholly unique, but since each combination of elements—size, style, color, and finish—is singular, the designs themselves can be considered custom. In truth, semi-custom might be a more accurate way to describe them.

the "stock" story

When you first start planning to build or remodel a kitchen, you may be surprised to learn that the cost of cabinetry can absorb more than half of your budget. Thus more and more homeowners are opting for stock cabinets—those they can select from catalogs or pull from the shelves of home center stores and high-end lumberyards.

When you start shopping, you will find that good-looking cabinets are available at every price point. Of course, you may not find the exact style or finish you want unless you are willing to spend a lot to get it. Or you may find you are interested in some of the so-called custom accessories that some cabinet lines include: lazy Susans, for example, spice shelves or drawers, pop-up small-appliance shelves, or beveled-glass door panels.

In each instance, cabinets considered semi-custom or custom modular may be your best choice. They will cost a little more than off-the-shelf cabinets but much less than those built entirely from scratch. Since most standard-size cabinets fit most standard-size kitchens, stock cabinets have become an acceptable choice for most homeowners, particularly those who want deluxe appliances and supremely durable work surfaces but need to find ways to hold down costs.

Whatever you finally order, make sure the quality of cabinet installation matches the quality of the product. Unless the fit is precise and accurate, your cabinets will never fully meet your design expectations or deliver the service you have a right to expect.

do a quality check

Before accepting any cabinet order, look carefully to see that joints are smooth and tight, with no visible staples, nail holes, or glue residue; that laminates are thick enough not to peel along the edges and corners, and that the drawers fit properly.

To ascertain drawer fit, try performing these tests:

- Pull each drawer a few inches out from the frame and try to move it from side to side; the less it wobbles, the more stable it is.

- Pull each drawer all the way out and push down; the drawer slide should not bend or bow but remain stable.

- Test to make sure each drawer moves in and out smoothly and with little effort.

photo credits

Cover: Anne Gummerson; back cover, clockwise from top: Eric Roth, Gridley & Graves, David Duncan Livingston. Page 6: Gridley and Graves; pages 8-11: Robert Polett; pages 12-15: Keller & Keller; pages 16-19: Storybook Studios; pages 20-23: John Bessler; pages 24-25: David Van Scott; pages 26-29: Jim Yochum; pages 30-35: David Duncan Livingston; pages 36-37: Gridley and Graves; pages 38-41: Olson Photographic, LLC; pages 42-45: Charles Schiller; pages 46-49: Robert Reck; pages 50-51: Sally Painter; pages 52-59: Gridley and Graves; page 60: Tria Giovan; pages 62-67: Alexandra Rowley; pages 68-71: J.R. Emmanuelli; pages 72-75: Gridley & Graves; pages 76-81: Alan Shortall; pages 82-83: David Duncan Livingston; pages 84-87: Eric Roth; pages 90-91: Matthew Millman; pages 92-99: Gridley & Graves; pages 100-103: Tim Fuller; pages 104-107: Mark Lohman; pages 108-111: David Duncan Livingston; pages 112-115: Anne Gummerson; pages 116-119: Evan Joseph.